C-169   CAREER EXAMINATION SERIES

This is your
PASSBOOK for...

Correction Sergeant

Test Preparation Study Guide
Questions & Answers

NATIONAL LEARNING CORPORATION®

COPYRIGHT NOTICE

This book is SOLELY intended for, is sold ONLY to, and its use is RESTRICTED to individual, bona fide applicants or candidates who qualify by virtue of having seriously filed applications for appropriate license, certificate, professional and/or promotional advancement, higher school matriculation, scholarship, or other legitimate requirements of education and/or governmental authorities.

This book is NOT intended for use, class instruction, tutoring, training, duplication, copying, reprinting, excerption, or adaptation, etc., by:

1) Other publishers
2) Proprietors and/or Instructors of "Coaching" and/or Preparatory Courses
3) Personnel and/or Training Divisions of commercial, industrial, and governmental organizations
4) Schools, colleges, or universities and/or their departments and staffs, including teachers and other personnel
5) Testing Agencies or Bureaus
6) Study groups which seek by the purchase of a single volume to copy and/or duplicate and/or adapt this material for use by the group as a whole without having purchased individual volumes for each of the members of the group
7) Et al.

Such persons would be in violation of appropriate Federal and State statutes.

PROVISION OF LICENSING AGREEMENTS – Recognized educational, commercial, industrial, and governmental institutions and organizations, and others legitimately engaged in educational pursuits, including training, testing, and measurement activities, may address request for a licensing agreement to the copyright owners, who will determine whether, and under what conditions, including fees and charges, the materials in this book may be used them. In other words, a licensing facility exists for the legitimate use of the material in this book on other than an individual basis. However, it is asseverated and affirmed here that the material in this book CANNOT be used without the receipt of the express permission of such a licensing agreement from the Publishers. Inquiries re licensing should be addressed to the company, attention rights and permissions department.

All rights reserved, including the right of reproduction in whole or in part, in any form or by any means, electronic or mechanical, including photocopying, recording, or by any information storage and retrieval system, without permission in writing from the Publisher.

Copyright © 2025 by
National Learning Corporation

212 Michael Drive, Syosset, NY 11791
(516) 921-8888 • www.passbooks.com
E-mail: info@passbooks.com

PASSBOOK® SERIES

THE *PASSBOOK® SERIES* has been created to prepare applicants and candidates for the ultimate academic battlefield – the examination room.

At some time in our lives, each and every one of us may be required to take an examination – for validation, matriculation, admission, qualification, registration, certification, or licensure.

Based on the assumption that every applicant or candidate has met the basic formal educational standards, has taken the required number of courses, and read the necessary texts, the *PASSBOOK® SERIES* furnishes the one special preparation which may assure passing with confidence, instead of failing with insecurity. Examination questions – together with answers – are furnished as the basic vehicle for study so that the mysteries of the examination and its compounding difficulties may be eliminated or diminished by a sure method.

This book is meant to help you pass your examination provided that you qualify and are serious in your objective.

The entire field is reviewed through the huge store of content information which is succinctly presented through a provocative and challenging approach – the question-and-answer method.

A climate of success is established by furnishing the correct answers at the end of each test.

You soon learn to recognize types of questions, forms of questions, and patterns of questioning. You may even begin to anticipate expected outcomes.

You perceive that many questions are repeated or adapted so that you can gain acute insights, which may enable you to score many sure points.

You learn how to confront new questions, or types of questions, and to attack them confidently and work out the correct answers.

You note objectives and emphases, and recognize pitfalls and dangers, so that you may make positive educational adjustments.

Moreover, you are kept fully informed in relation to new concepts, methods, practices, and directions in the field.

You discover that you are actually taking the examination all the time: you are preparing for the examination by "taking" an examination, not by reading extraneous and/or supererogatory textbooks.

In short, this PASSBOOK®, used directedly, should be an important factor in helping you to pass your test.

CORRECTION SERGEANT

DUTIES:
　　Under the general supervision of a Correction Lieutenant, an employee in this class supervises the activities of lower-level officers on an assigned shift. The work involves responsibility for supervising the work of Correction Officers and insuring enforcement of rules and regulations governing security, conduct, discipline, safety and the general well being of inmates and staff in the county correctional facility. Work procedures are well defined but incumbents must be alert to possibilities of emergency situations arising and exercise sound judgment when problems occur. The work is performed under general supervision of a higher ranking officer with leeway allowed for the exercise of independent judgment in dealing with day to day situations in the facility. Supervision is exercised over the work of an assigned group of Correction Officers. Does related work as required.

SCOPE OF THE EXAMINATION:
The written test will cover knowledge, skills, and/or abilities in such areas as:
1. Administrative supervision;
2. State correction laws, rules, regulations and minimum standards governing local correctional facilities and jails;
3. Coordinating appropriate responses to emergencies, disturbances and other unusual situations;
4. Custody, security and building maintenance procedures in correctional facilities; and
5. Preparing written material.

HOW TO TAKE A TEST

I. YOU MUST PASS AN EXAMINATION

A. *WHAT EVERY CANDIDATE SHOULD KNOW*

Examination applicants often ask us for help in preparing for the written test. What can I study in advance? What kinds of questions will be asked? How will the test be given? How will the papers be graded?

As an applicant for a civil service examination, you may be wondering about some of these things. Our purpose here is to suggest effective methods of advance study and to describe civil service examinations.

Your chances for success on this examination can be increased if you know how to prepare. Those "pre-examination jitters" can be reduced if you know what to expect. You can even experience an adventure in good citizenship if you know why civil service exams are given.

B. *WHY ARE CIVIL SERVICE EXAMINATIONS GIVEN?*

Civil service examinations are important to you in two ways. As a citizen, you want public jobs filled by employees who know how to do their work. As a job seeker, you want a fair chance to compete for that job on an equal footing with other candidates. The best-known means of accomplishing this two-fold goal is the competitive examination.

Exams are widely publicized throughout the nation. They may be administered for jobs in federal, state, city, municipal, town or village governments or agencies.

Any citizen may apply, with some limitations, such as the age or residence of applicants. Your experience and education may be reviewed to see whether you meet the requirements for the particular examination. When these requirements exist, they are reasonable and applied consistently to all applicants. Thus, a competitive examination may cause you some uneasiness now, but it is your privilege and safeguard.

C. *HOW ARE CIVIL SERVICE EXAMS DEVELOPED?*

Examinations are carefully written by trained technicians who are specialists in the field known as "psychological measurement," in consultation with recognized authorities in the field of work that the test will cover. These experts recommend the subject matter areas or skills to be tested; only those knowledges or skills important to your success on the job are included. The most reliable books and source materials available are used as references. Together, the experts and technicians judge the difficulty level of the questions.

Test technicians know how to phrase questions so that the problem is clearly stated. Their ethics do not permit "trick" or "catch" questions. Questions may have been tried out on sample groups, or subjected to statistical analysis, to determine their usefulness.

Written tests are often used in combination with performance tests, ratings of training and experience, and oral interviews. All of these measures combine to form the best-known means of finding the right person for the right job.

II. HOW TO PASS THE WRITTEN TEST

A. NATURE OF THE EXAMINATION

To prepare intelligently for civil service examinations, you should know how they differ from school examinations you have taken. In school you were assigned certain definite pages to read or subjects to cover. The examination questions were quite detailed and usually emphasized memory. Civil service exams, on the other hand, try to discover your present ability to perform the duties of a position, plus your potentiality to learn these duties. In other words, a civil service exam attempts to predict how successful you will be. Questions cover such a broad area that they cannot be as minute and detailed as school exam questions.

In the public service similar kinds of work, or positions, are grouped together in one "class." This process is known as *position-classification*. All the positions in a class are paid according to the salary range for that class. One class title covers all of these positions, and they are all tested by the same examination.

B. FOUR BASIC STEPS

1) Study the announcement

How, then, can you know what subjects to study? Our best answer is: "Learn as much as possible about the class of positions for which you've applied." The exam will test the knowledge, skills and abilities needed to do the work.

Your most valuable source of information about the position you want is the official exam announcement. This announcement lists the training and experience qualifications. Check these standards and apply only if you come reasonably close to meeting them.

The brief description of the position in the examination announcement offers some clues to the subjects which will be tested. Think about the job itself. Review the duties in your mind. Can you perform them, or are there some in which you are rusty? Fill in the blank spots in your preparation.

Many jurisdictions preview the written test in the exam announcement by including a section called "Knowledge and Abilities Required," "Scope of the Examination," or some similar heading. Here you will find out specifically what fields will be tested.

2) Review your own background

Once you learn in general what the position is all about, and what you need to know to do the work, ask yourself which subjects you already know fairly well and which need improvement. You may wonder whether to concentrate on improving your strong areas or on building some background in your fields of weakness. When the announcement has specified "some knowledge" or "considerable knowledge," or has used adjectives like "beginning principles of…" or "advanced … methods," you can get a clue as to the number and difficulty of questions to be asked in any given field. More questions, and hence broader coverage, would be included for those subjects which are more important in the work. Now weigh your strengths and weaknesses against the job requirements and prepare accordingly.

3) Determine the level of the position

Another way to tell how intensively you should prepare is to understand the level of the job for which you are applying. Is it the entering level? In other words, is this the position in which beginners in a field of work are hired? Or is it an intermediate or advanced level? Sometimes this is indicated by such words as "Junior" or "Senior" in the class title. Other jurisdictions use Roman numerals to designate the level – Clerk I, Clerk II, for example. The word "Supervisor" sometimes appears in the title. If the level is not indicated by the title, check the description of duties. Will you be working under very close supervision, or will you have responsibility for independent decisions in this work?

4) Choose appropriate study materials

Now that you know the subjects to be examined and the relative amount of each subject to be covered, you can choose suitable study materials. For beginning level jobs, or even advanced ones, if you have a pronounced weakness in some aspect of your training, read a modern, standard textbook in that field. Be sure it is up to date and has general coverage. Such books are normally available at your library, and the librarian will be glad to help you locate one. For entry-level positions, questions of appropriate difficulty are chosen – neither highly advanced questions, nor those too simple. Such questions require careful thought but not advanced training.

If the position for which you are applying is technical or advanced, you will read more advanced, specialized material. If you are already familiar with the basic principles of your field, elementary textbooks would waste your time. Concentrate on advanced textbooks and technical periodicals. Think through the concepts and review difficult problems in your field.

These are all general sources. You can get more ideas on your own initiative, following these leads. For example, training manuals and publications of the government agency which employs workers in your field can be useful, particularly for technical and professional positions. A letter or visit to the government department involved may result in more specific study suggestions, and certainly will provide you with a more definite idea of the exact nature of the position you are seeking.

III. KINDS OF TESTS

Tests are used for purposes other than measuring knowledge and ability to perform specified duties. For some positions, it is equally important to test ability to make adjustments to new situations or to profit from training. In others, basic mental abilities not dependent on information are essential. Questions which test these things may not appear as pertinent to the duties of the position as those which test for knowledge and information. Yet they are often highly important parts of a fair examination. For very general questions, it is almost impossible to help you direct your study efforts. What we can do is to point out some of the more common of these general abilities needed in public service positions and describe some typical questions.

1) General information

Broad, general information has been found useful for predicting job success in some kinds of work. This is tested in a variety of ways, from vocabulary lists to questions about current events. Basic background in some field of work, such as sociology or economics, may be sampled in a group of questions. Often these are principles which have become familiar to most persons through exposure rather than through formal training. It is difficult to advise you how to study for these questions; being alert to the world around you is our best suggestion.

2) Verbal ability

An example of an ability needed in many positions is verbal or language ability. Verbal ability is, in brief, the ability to use and understand words. Vocabulary and grammar tests are typical measures of this ability. Reading comprehension or paragraph interpretation questions are common in many kinds of civil service tests. You are given a paragraph of written material and asked to find its central meaning.

3) Numerical ability

Number skills can be tested by the familiar arithmetic problem, by checking paired lists of numbers to see which are alike and which are different, or by interpreting charts and graphs. In the latter test, a graph may be printed in the test booklet which you are asked to use as the basis for answering questions.

4) Observation

A popular test for law-enforcement positions is the observation test. A picture is shown to you for several minutes, then taken away. Questions about the picture test your ability to observe both details and larger elements.

5) Following directions

In many positions in the public service, the employee must be able to carry out written instructions dependably and accurately. You may be given a chart with several columns, each column listing a variety of information. The questions require you to carry out directions involving the information given in the chart.

6) Skills and aptitudes

Performance tests effectively measure some manual skills and aptitudes. When the skill is one in which you are trained, such as typing or shorthand, you can practice. These tests are often very much like those given in business school or high school courses. For many of the other skills and aptitudes, however, no short-time preparation can be made. Skills and abilities natural to you or that you have developed throughout your lifetime are being tested.

Many of the general questions just described provide all the data needed to answer the questions and ask you to use your reasoning ability to find the answers. Your best preparation for these tests, as well as for tests of facts and ideas, is to be at your physical and mental best. You, no doubt, have your own methods of getting into an exam-taking mood and keeping "in shape." The next section lists some ideas on this subject.

IV. KINDS OF QUESTIONS

Only rarely is the "essay" question, which you answer in narrative form, used in civil service tests. Civil service tests are usually of the short-answer type. Full instructions for answering these questions will be given to you at the examination. But in case this is your first experience with short-answer questions and separate answer sheets, here is what you need to know:

1) Multiple-choice Questions

Most popular of the short-answer questions is the "multiple choice" or "best answer" question. It can be used, for example, to test for factual knowledge, ability to solve problems or judgment in meeting situations found at work.

A multiple-choice question is normally one of three types—
- It can begin with an incomplete statement followed by several possible endings. You are to find the one ending which *best* completes the statement, although some of the others may not be entirely wrong.
- It can also be a complete statement in the form of a question which is answered by choosing one of the statements listed.

- It can be in the form of a problem – again you select the best answer.

Here is an example of a multiple-choice question with a discussion which should give you some clues as to the method for choosing the right answer:

When an employee has a complaint about his assignment, the action which will *best* help him overcome his difficulty is to
- A. discuss his difficulty with his coworkers
- B. take the problem to the head of the organization
- C. take the problem to the person who gave him the assignment
- D. say nothing to anyone about his complaint

In answering this question, you should study each of the choices to find which is best. Consider choice "A" – Certainly an employee may discuss his complaint with fellow employees, but no change or improvement can result, and the complaint remains unresolved. Choice "B" is a poor choice since the head of the organization probably does not know what assignment you have been given, and taking your problem to him is known as "going over the head" of the supervisor. The supervisor, or person who made the assignment, is the person who can clarify it or correct any injustice. Choice "C" is, therefore, correct. To say nothing, as in choice "D," is unwise. Supervisors have and interest in knowing the problems employees are facing, and the employee is seeking a solution to his problem.

2) True/False Questions

The "true/false" or "right/wrong" form of question is sometimes used. Here a complete statement is given. Your job is to decide whether the statement is right or wrong.

SAMPLE: A roaming cell-phone call to a nearby city costs less than a non-roaming call to a distant city.

This statement is wrong, or false, since roaming calls are more expensive.

This is not a complete list of all possible question forms, although most of the others are variations of these common types. You will always get complete directions for answering questions. Be sure you understand *how* to mark your answers – ask questions until you do.

V. RECORDING YOUR ANSWERS

Computer terminals are used more and more today for many different kinds of exams.

For an examination with very few applicants, you may be told to record your answers in the test booklet itself. Separate answer sheets are much more common. If this separate answer sheet is to be scored by machine – and this is often the case – it is highly important that you mark your answers correctly in order to get credit.

An electronic scoring machine is often used in civil service offices because of the speed with which papers can be scored. Machine-scored answer sheets must be marked with a pencil, which will be given to you. This pencil has a high graphite content which responds to the electronic scoring machine. As a matter of fact, stray dots may register as answers, so do not let your pencil rest on the answer sheet while you are pondering the correct answer. Also, if your pencil lead breaks or is otherwise defective, ask for another.

Since the answer sheet will be dropped in a slot in the scoring machine, be careful not to bend the corners or get the paper crumpled.

The answer sheet normally has five vertical columns of numbers, with 30 numbers to a column. These numbers correspond to the question numbers in your test booklet. After each number, going across the page are four or five pairs of dotted lines. These short dotted lines have small letters or numbers above them. The first two pairs may also have a "T" or "F" above the letters. This indicates that the first two pairs only are to be used if the questions are of the true-false type. If the questions are multiple choice, disregard the "T" and "F" and pay attention only to the small letters or numbers.

Answer your questions in the manner of the sample that follows:

32. The largest city in the United States is
    A. Washington, D.C.
    B. New York City
    C. Chicago
    D. Detroit
    E. San Francisco

1) Choose the answer you think is best. (New York City is the largest, so "B" is correct.)
2) Find the row of dotted lines numbered the same as the question you are answering. (Find row number 32)
3) Find the pair of dotted lines corresponding to the answer. (Find the pair of lines under the mark "B.")
4) Make a solid black mark between the dotted lines.

VI. BEFORE THE TEST

Common sense will help you find procedures to follow to get ready for an examination. Too many of us, however, overlook these sensible measures. Indeed, nervousness and fatigue have been found to be the most serious reasons why applicants fail to do their best on civil service tests. Here is a list of reminders:

- Begin your preparation early – Don't wait until the last minute to go scurrying around for books and materials or to find out what the position is all about.
- Prepare continuously – An hour a night for a week is better than an all-night cram session. This has been definitely established. What is more, a night a week for a month will return better dividends than crowding your study into a shorter period of time.
- Locate the place of the exam – You have been sent a notice telling you when and where to report for the examination. If the location is in a different town or otherwise unfamiliar to you, it would be well to inquire the best route and learn something about the building.
- Relax the night before the test – Allow your mind to rest. Do not study at all that night. Plan some mild recreation or diversion; then go to bed early and get a good night's sleep.
- Get up early enough to make a leisurely trip to the place for the test – This way unforeseen events, traffic snarls, unfamiliar buildings, etc. will not upset you.
- Dress comfortably – A written test is not a fashion show. You will be known by number and not by name, so wear something comfortable.

- Leave excess paraphernalia at home – Shopping bags and odd bundles will get in your way. You need bring only the items mentioned in the official notice you received; usually everything you need is provided. Do not bring reference books to the exam. They will only confuse those last minutes and be taken away from you when in the test room.
- Arrive somewhat ahead of time – If because of transportation schedules you must get there very early, bring a newspaper or magazine to take your mind off yourself while waiting.
- Locate the examination room – When you have found the proper room, you will be directed to the seat or part of the room where you will sit. Sometimes you are given a sheet of instructions to read while you are waiting. Do not fill out any forms until you are told to do so; just read them and be prepared.
- Relax and prepare to listen to the instructions
- If you have any physical problem that may keep you from doing your best, be sure to tell the test administrator. If you are sick or in poor health, you really cannot do your best on the exam. You can come back and take the test some other time.

VII. AT THE TEST

The day of the test is here and you have the test booklet in your hand. The temptation to get going is very strong. Caution! There is more to success than knowing the right answers. You must know how to identify your papers and understand variations in the type of short-answer question used in this particular examination. Follow these suggestions for maximum results from your efforts:

1) Cooperate with the monitor

The test administrator has a duty to create a situation in which you can be as much at ease as possible. He will give instructions, tell you when to begin, check to see that you are marking your answer sheet correctly, and so on. He is not there to guard you, although he will see that your competitors do not take unfair advantage. He wants to help you do your best.

2) Listen to all instructions

Don't jump the gun! Wait until you understand all directions. In most civil service tests you get more time than you need to answer the questions. So don't be in a hurry. Read each word of instructions until you clearly understand the meaning. Study the examples, listen to all announcements and follow directions. Ask questions if you do not understand what to do.

3) Identify your papers

Civil service exams are usually identified by number only. You will be assigned a number; you must not put your name on your test papers. Be sure to copy your number correctly. Since more than one exam may be given, copy your exact examination title.

4) Plan your time

Unless you are told that a test is a "speed" or "rate of work" test, speed itself is usually not important. Time enough to answer all the questions will be provided, but this does not mean that you have all day. An overall time limit has been set. Divide the total time (in minutes) by the number of questions to determine the approximate time you have for each question.

5) Do not linger over difficult questions

If you come across a difficult question, mark it with a paper clip (useful to have along) and come back to it when you have been through the booklet. One caution if you do this — be sure to skip a number on your answer sheet as well. Check often to be sure that you have not lost your place and that you are marking in the row numbered the same as the question you are answering.

6) Read the questions

Be sure you know what the question asks! Many capable people are unsuccessful because they failed to *read* the questions correctly.

7) Answer all questions

Unless you have been instructed that a penalty will be deducted for incorrect answers, it is better to guess than to omit a question.

8) Speed tests

It is often better NOT to guess on speed tests. It has been found that on timed tests people are tempted to spend the last few seconds before time is called in marking answers at random — without even reading them — in the hope of picking up a few extra points. To discourage this practice, the instructions may warn you that your score will be "corrected" for guessing. That is, a penalty will be applied. The incorrect answers will be deducted from the correct ones, or some other penalty formula will be used.

9) Review your answers

If you finish before time is called, go back to the questions you guessed or omitted to give them further thought. Review other answers if you have time.

10) Return your test materials

If you are ready to leave before others have finished or time is called, take ALL your materials to the monitor and leave quietly. Never take any test material with you. The monitor can discover whose papers are not complete, and taking a test booklet may be grounds for disqualification.

VIII. EXAMINATION TECHNIQUES

1) Read the general instructions carefully. These are usually printed on the first page of the exam booklet. As a rule, these instructions refer to the timing of the examination; the fact that you should not start work until the signal and must stop work at a signal, etc. If there are any *special* instructions, such as a choice of questions to be answered, make sure that you note this instruction carefully.

2) When you are ready to start work on the examination, that is as soon as the signal has been given, read the instructions to each question booklet, underline any key words or phrases, such as *least, best, outline, describe* and the like. In this way you will tend to answer as requested rather than discover on reviewing your paper that you *listed without describing*, that you selected the *worst* choice rather than the *best* choice, etc.

3) If the examination is of the objective or multiple-choice type – that is, each question will also give a series of possible answers: A, B, C or D, and you are called upon to select the best answer and write the letter next to that answer on your answer paper – it is advisable to start answering each question in turn. There may be anywhere from 50 to 100 such questions in the three or four hours allotted and you can see how much time would be taken if you read through all the questions before beginning to answer any. Furthermore, if you come across a question or group of questions which you know would be difficult to answer, it would undoubtedly affect your handling of all the other questions.

4) If the examination is of the essay type and contains but a few questions, it is a moot point as to whether you should read all the questions before starting to answer any one. Of course, if you are given a choice – say five out of seven and the like – then it is essential to read all the questions so you can eliminate the two that are most difficult. If, however, you are asked to answer all the questions, there may be danger in trying to answer the easiest one first because you may find that you will spend too much time on it. The best technique is to answer the first question, then proceed to the second, etc.

5) Time your answers. Before the exam begins, write down the time it started, then add the time allowed for the examination and write down the time it must be completed, then divide the time available somewhat as follows:
    - If 3-1/2 hours are allowed, that would be 210 minutes. If you have 80 objective-type questions, that would be an average of 2-1/2 minutes per question. Allow yourself no more than 2 minutes per question, or a total of 160 minutes, which will permit about 50 minutes to review.
    - If for the time allotment of 210 minutes there are 7 essay questions to answer, that would average about 30 minutes a question. Give yourself only 25 minutes per question so that you have about 35 minutes to review.

6) The most important instruction is to *read each question* and make sure you know what is wanted. The second most important instruction is to *time yourself properly* so that you answer every question. The third most important instruction is to *answer every question*. Guess if you have to but include something for each question. Remember that you will receive no credit for a blank and will probably receive some credit if you write something in answer to an essay question. If you guess a letter – say "B" for a multiple-choice question – you may have guessed right. If you leave a blank as an answer to a multiple-choice question, the examiners may respect your feelings but it will not add a point to your score. Some exams may penalize you for wrong answers, so in such cases *only*, you may not want to guess unless you have some basis for your answer.

7) Suggestions
    a. Objective-type questions
        1. Examine the question booklet for proper sequence of pages and questions
        2. Read all instructions carefully
        3. Skip any question which seems too difficult; return to it after all other questions have been answered
        4. Apportion your time properly; do not spend too much time on any single question or group of questions

5. Note and underline key words – *all, most, fewest, least, best, worst, same, opposite,* etc.
6. Pay particular attention to negatives
7. Note unusual option, e.g., unduly long, short, complex, different or similar in content to the body of the question
8. Observe the use of "hedging" words – *probably, may, most likely,* etc.
9. Make sure that your answer is put next to the same number as the question
10. Do not second-guess unless you have good reason to believe the second answer is definitely more correct
11. Cross out original answer if you decide another answer is more accurate; do not erase until you are ready to hand your paper in
12. Answer all questions; guess unless instructed otherwise
13. Leave time for review

  b. Essay questions
1. Read each question carefully
2. Determine exactly what is wanted. Underline key words or phrases.
3. Decide on outline or paragraph answer
4. Include many different points and elements unless asked to develop any one or two points or elements
5. Show impartiality by giving pros and cons unless directed to select one side only
6. Make and write down any assumptions you find necessary to answer the questions
7. Watch your English, grammar, punctuation and choice of words
8. Time your answers; don't crowd material

8) Answering the essay question

Most essay questions can be answered by framing the specific response around several key words or ideas. Here are a few such key words or ideas:

M's: manpower, materials, methods, money, management
P's: purpose, program, policy, plan, procedure, practice, problems, pitfalls, personnel, public relations

  a. Six basic steps in handling problems:
1. Preliminary plan and background development
2. Collect information, data and facts
3. Analyze and interpret information, data and facts
4. Analyze and develop solutions as well as make recommendations
5. Prepare report and sell recommendations
6. Install recommendations and follow up effectiveness

  b. Pitfalls to avoid
1. *Taking things for granted* – A statement of the situation does not necessarily imply that each of the elements is necessarily true; for example, a complaint may be invalid and biased so that all that can be taken for granted is that a complaint has been registered

2. *Considering only one side of a situation* – Wherever possible, indicate several alternatives and then point out the reasons you selected the best one
3. *Failing to indicate follow up* – Whenever your answer indicates action on your part, make certain that you will take proper follow-up action to see how successful your recommendations, procedures or actions turn out to be
4. *Taking too long in answering any single question* – Remember to time your answers properly

IX. AFTER THE TEST

Scoring procedures differ in detail among civil service jurisdictions although the general principles are the same. Whether the papers are hand-scored or graded by machine we have described, they are nearly always graded by number. That is, the person who marks the paper knows only the number – never the name – of the applicant. Not until all the papers have been graded will they be matched with names. If other tests, such as training and experience or oral interview ratings have been given, scores will be combined. Different parts of the examination usually have different weights. For example, the written test might count 60 percent of the final grade, and a rating of training and experience 40 percent. In many jurisdictions, veterans will have a certain number of points added to their grades.

After the final grade has been determined, the names are placed in grade order and an eligible list is established. There are various methods for resolving ties between those who get the same final grade – probably the most common is to place first the name of the person whose application was received first. Job offers are made from the eligible list in the order the names appear on it. You will be notified of your grade and your rank as soon as all these computations have been made. This will be done as rapidly as possible.

People who are found to meet the requirements in the announcement are called "eligibles." Their names are put on a list of eligible candidates. An eligible's chances of getting a job depend on how high he stands on this list and how fast agencies are filling jobs from the list.

When a job is to be filled from a list of eligibles, the agency asks for the names of people on the list of eligibles for that job. When the civil service commission receives this request, it sends to the agency the names of the three people highest on this list. Or, if the job to be filled has specialized requirements, the office sends the agency the names of the top three persons who meet these requirements from the general list.

The appointing officer makes a choice from among the three people whose names were sent to him. If the selected person accepts the appointment, the names of the others are put back on the list to be considered for future openings.

That is the rule in hiring from all kinds of eligible lists, whether they are for typist, carpenter, chemist, or something else. For every vacancy, the appointing officer has his choice of any one of the top three eligibles on the list. This explains why the person whose name is on top of the list sometimes does not get an appointment when some of the persons lower on the list do. If the appointing officer chooses the second or third eligible, the No. 1 eligible does not get a job at once, but stays on the list until he is appointed or the list is terminated.

X. HOW TO PASS THE INTERVIEW TEST

The examination for which you applied requires an oral interview test. You have already taken the written test and you are now being called for the interview test – the final part of the formal examination.

You may think that it is not possible to prepare for an interview test and that there are no procedures to follow during an interview. Our purpose is to point out some things you can do in advance that will help you and some good rules to follow and pitfalls to avoid while you are being interviewed.

What is an interview supposed to test?

The written examination is designed to test the technical knowledge and competence of the candidate; the oral is designed to evaluate intangible qualities, not readily measured otherwise, and to establish a list showing the relative fitness of each candidate – as measured against his competitors – for the position sought. Scoring is not on the basis of "right" and "wrong," but on a sliding scale of values ranging from "not passable" to "outstanding." As a matter of fact, it is possible to achieve a relatively low score without a single "incorrect" answer because of evident weakness in the qualities being measured.

Occasionally, an examination may consist entirely of an oral test – either an individual or a group oral. In such cases, information is sought concerning the technical knowledges and abilities of the candidate, since there has been no written examination for this purpose. More commonly, however, an oral test is used to supplement a written examination.

Who conducts interviews?

The composition of oral boards varies among different jurisdictions. In nearly all, a representative of the personnel department serves as chairman. One of the members of the board may be a representative of the department in which the candidate would work. In some cases, "outside experts" are used, and, frequently, a businessman or some other representative of the general public is asked to serve. Labor and management or other special groups may be represented. The aim is to secure the services of experts in the appropriate field.

However the board is composed, it is a good idea (and not at all improper or unethical) to ascertain in advance of the interview who the members are and what groups they represent. When you are introduced to them, you will have some idea of their backgrounds and interests, and at least you will not stutter and stammer over their names.

What should be done before the interview?

While knowledge about the board members is useful and takes some of the surprise element out of the interview, there is other preparation which is more substantive. It *is* possible to prepare for an oral interview – in several ways:

1) Keep a copy of your application and review it carefully before the interview

This may be the only document before the oral board, and the starting point of the interview. Know what education and experience you have listed there, and the sequence and dates of all of it. Sometimes the board will ask you to review the highlights of your experience for them; you should not have to hem and haw doing it.

2) Study the class specification and the examination announcement

Usually, the oral board has one or both of these to guide them. The qualities, characteristics or knowledges required by the position sought are stated in these documents. They offer valuable clues as to the nature of the oral interview. For example, if the job involves supervisory responsibilities, the announcement will usually indicate that knowledge of modern supervisory methods and the qualifications of the candidate as a supervisor will be tested. If so, you can expect such questions, frequently in the form of a hypothetical situation which you are expected to solve. NEVER go into an oral without knowledge of the duties and responsibilities of the job you seek.

3) Think through each qualification required

Try to visualize the kind of questions you would ask if you were a board member. How well could you answer them? Try especially to appraise your own knowledge and background in each area, *measured against the job sought*, and identify any areas in which you are weak. Be critical and realistic – do not flatter yourself.

4) Do some general reading in areas in which you feel you may be weak

For example, if the job involves supervision and your past experience has NOT, some general reading in supervisory methods and practices, particularly in the field of human relations, might be useful. Do NOT study agency procedures or detailed manuals. The oral board will be testing your understanding and capacity, not your memory.

5) Get a good night's sleep and watch your general health and mental attitude

You will want a clear head at the interview. Take care of a cold or any other minor ailment, and of course, no hangovers.

What should be done on the day of the interview?

Now comes the day of the interview itself. Give yourself plenty of time to get there. Plan to arrive somewhat ahead of the scheduled time, particularly if your appointment is in the fore part of the day. If a previous candidate fails to appear, the board might be ready for you a bit early. By early afternoon an oral board is almost invariably behind schedule if there are many candidates, and you may have to wait. Take along a book or magazine to read, or your application to review, but leave any extraneous material in the waiting room when you go in for your interview. In any event, relax and compose yourself.

The matter of dress is important. The board is forming impressions about you – from your experience, your manners, your attitude, and your appearance. Give your personal appearance careful attention. Dress your best, but not your flashiest. Choose conservative, appropriate clothing, and be sure it is immaculate. This is a business interview, and your appearance should indicate that you regard it as such. Besides, being well groomed and properly dressed will help boost your confidence.

Sooner or later, someone will call your name and escort you into the interview room. *This is it.* From here on you are on your own. It is too late for any more preparation. But remember, you asked for this opportunity to prove your fitness, and you are here because your request was granted.

What happens when you go in?

The usual sequence of events will be as follows: The clerk (who is often the board stenographer) will introduce you to the chairman of the oral board, who will introduce you to the other members of the board. Acknowledge the introductions before you sit down. Do not be surprised if you find a microphone facing you or a stenotypist sitting by. Oral interviews are usually recorded in the event of an appeal or other review.

Usually the chairman of the board will open the interview by reviewing the highlights of your education and work experience from your application – primarily for the benefit of the other members of the board, as well as to get the material into the record. Do not interrupt or comment unless there is an error or significant misinterpretation; if that is the case, do not hesitate. But do not quibble about insignificant matters. Also, he will usually ask you some question about your education, experience or your present job – partly to get you to start talking and to establish the interviewing "rapport." He may start the actual questioning, or turn it over to one of the other members. Frequently, each member undertakes the questioning on a particular area, one in which he is perhaps most competent, so you can expect each member to participate in the examination. Because time is limited, you may also expect some rather abrupt switches in the direction the questioning takes, so do not be upset by it. Normally, a board member will not pursue a single line of questioning unless he discovers a particular strength or weakness.

After each member has participated, the chairman will usually ask whether any member has any further questions, then will ask you if you have anything you wish to add. Unless you are expecting this question, it may floor you. Worse, it may start you off on an extended, extemporaneous speech. The board is not usually seeking more information. The question is principally to offer you a last opportunity to present further qualifications or to indicate that you have nothing to add. So, if you feel that a significant qualification or characteristic has been overlooked, it is proper to point it out in a sentence or so. Do not compliment the board on the thoroughness of their examination – they have been sketchy, and you know it. If you wish, merely say, "No thank you, I have nothing further to add." This is a point where you can "talk yourself out" of a good impression or fail to present an important bit of information. Remember, *you close the interview yourself.*

The chairman will then say, "That is all, Mr. _____, thank you." Do not be startled; the interview is over, and quicker than you think. Thank him, gather your belongings and take your leave. Save your sigh of relief for the other side of the door.

How to put your best foot forward

Throughout this entire process, you may feel that the board individually and collectively is trying to pierce your defenses, seek out your hidden weaknesses and embarrass and confuse you. Actually, this is not true. They are obliged to make an appraisal of your qualifications for the job you are seeking, and they want to see you in your best light. Remember, they must interview all candidates and a non-cooperative candidate may become a failure in spite of their best efforts to bring out his qualifications. Here are 15 suggestions that will help you:

1) Be natural – Keep your attitude confident, not cocky

If you are not confident that you can do the job, do not expect the board to be. Do not apologize for your weaknesses, try to bring out your strong points. The board is interested in a positive, not negative, presentation. Cockiness will antagonize any board member and make him wonder if you are covering up a weakness by a false show of strength.

2) Get comfortable, but don't lounge or sprawl

Sit erectly but not stiffly. A careless posture may lead the board to conclude that you are careless in other things, or at least that you are not impressed by the importance of the occasion. Either conclusion is natural, even if incorrect. Do not fuss with your clothing, a pencil or an ashtray. Your hands may occasionally be useful to emphasize a point; do not let them become a point of distraction.

3) Do not wisecrack or make small talk

This is a serious situation, and your attitude should show that you consider it as such. Further, the time of the board is limited – they do not want to waste it, and neither should you.

4) Do not exaggerate your experience or abilities

In the first place, from information in the application or other interviews and sources, the board may know more about you than you think. Secondly, you probably will not get away with it. An experienced board is rather adept at spotting such a situation, so do not take the chance.

5) If you know a board member, do not make a point of it, yet do not hide it

Certainly you are not fooling him, and probably not the other members of the board. Do not try to take advantage of your acquaintanceship – it will probably do you little good.

6) Do not dominate the interview

Let the board do that. They will give you the clues – do not assume that you have to do all the talking. Realize that the board has a number of questions to ask you, and do not try to take up all the interview time by showing off your extensive knowledge of the answer to the first one.

7) Be attentive

You only have 20 minutes or so, and you should keep your attention at its sharpest throughout. When a member is addressing a problem or question to you, give him your undivided attention. Address your reply principally to him, but do not exclude the other board members.

8) Do not interrupt

A board member may be stating a problem for you to analyze. He will ask you a question when the time comes. Let him state the problem, and wait for the question.

9) Make sure you understand the question

Do not try to answer until you are sure what the question is. If it is not clear, restate it in your own words or ask the board member to clarify it for you. However, do not haggle about minor elements.

10) Reply promptly but not hastily

A common entry on oral board rating sheets is "candidate responded readily," or "candidate hesitated in replies." Respond as promptly and quickly as you can, but do not jump to a hasty, ill-considered answer.

11) Do not be peremptory in your answers

A brief answer is proper – but do not fire your answer back. That is a losing game from your point of view. The board member can probably ask questions much faster than you can answer them.

12) Do not try to create the answer you think the board member wants

He is interested in what kind of mind you have and how it works – not in playing games. Furthermore, he can usually spot this practice and will actually grade you down on it.

13) Do not switch sides in your reply merely to agree with a board member

Frequently, a member will take a contrary position merely to draw you out and to see if you are willing and able to defend your point of view. Do not start a debate, yet do not surrender a good position. If a position is worth taking, it is worth defending.

14) Do not be afraid to admit an error in judgment if you are shown to be wrong

The board knows that you are forced to reply without any opportunity for careful consideration. Your answer may be demonstrably wrong. If so, admit it and get on with the interview.

15) Do not dwell at length on your present job

The opening question may relate to your present assignment. Answer the question but do not go into an extended discussion. You are being examined for a *new* job, not your present one. As a matter of fact, try to phrase ALL your answers in terms of the job for which you are being examined.

Basis of Rating

Probably you will forget most of these "do's" and "don'ts" when you walk into the oral interview room. Even remembering them all will not ensure you a passing grade. Perhaps you did not have the qualifications in the first place. But remembering them will help you to put your best foot forward, without treading on the toes of the board members.

Rumor and popular opinion to the contrary notwithstanding, an oral board wants you to make the best appearance possible. They know you are under pressure – but they also want to see how you respond to it as a guide to what your reaction would be under the pressures of the job you seek. They will be influenced by the degree of poise you display, the personal traits you show and the manner in which you respond.

ABOUT THIS BOOK

This book contains tests divided into Examination Sections. Go through each test, answering every question in the margin. We have also attached a sample answer sheet at the back of the book that can be removed and used. At the end of each test look at the answer key and check your answers. On the ones you got wrong, look at the right answer choice and learn. Do not fill in the answers first. Do not memorize the questions and answers, but understand the answer and principles involved. On your test, the questions will likely be different from the samples. Questions are changed and new ones added. If you understand these past questions you should have success with any changes that arise. Tests may consist of several types of questions. We have additional books on each subject should more study be advisable or necessary for you. Finally, the more you study, the better prepared you will be. This book is intended to be the last thing you study before you walk into the examination room. Prior study of relevant texts is also recommended. NLC publishes some of these in our Fundamental Series. Knowledge and good sense are important factors in passing your exam. Good luck also helps. So now study this Passbook, absorb the material contained within and take that knowledge into the examination. Then do your best to pass that exam.

EXAMINATION SECTION

EXAMINATION SECTION
TEST 1

DIRECTIONS: Each question or incomplete statement is followed by several suggested answers or completions. Select the one that BEST answers the question or completes the statement. *PRINT THE LETTER OF THE CORRECT ANSWER IN THE SPACE AT THE RIGHT.*

1. Assume that you are a supervisor. A newly appointed correction officer asks you what action he should take if, when patrolling a cell block at night, he notices that a prisoner has suddenly been taken violently ill.
Of the following, the BEST advice for you to give this correction officer is that he should

   A. check carefully on the circumstances of the case before opening the cell
   B. open the cell immediately and apply first aid as soon as possible
   C. open the cell immediately, examine the inmate quickly, and summon a doctor if the illness seems real
   D. summon another guard before opening the cell
   E. ask the inmate what the trouble is before summoning a doctor

   1.____

2. Suppose that a correction officer, coming on duty, reports to you that a prisoner is missing from the cell block.
Of the following, the BEST reason for sounding an alarm immediately, before checking the officer's count, is that

   A. there may have been an error in the count
   B. the escaped prisoner may have had an accomplice
   C. there is no indication how long the inmate may have been missing from his cell
   D. responsibility for the escape should be fixed immediately
   E. the inmate may still be on the prison grounds

   2.____

3. An institution with competent superiors will be an institution well-run.
Of the following, the BEST justification for this statement is that

   A. the duties of superiors, although often supervisory, are essentially sustodial
   B. competent supervision is usually reflected by competent performance of duties
   C. if subordinates are inefficient, competent supervision becomes increasingly difficult
   D. even competent supervisors need the cooperation of their superior officers
   E. competent superiors are usually policy-makers as well as supervisors

   3.____

4. Assume that, while you are on duty, an inmate falls to the ground in an epileptic fit.
Of the following, the MOST important step for you to take first is to

   A. take precautions to avoid having the inmate go into a state of shock
   B. apply artificial respiration
   C. take precautions to prevent the inmate from choking
   D. examine the inmate for broken bones before moving him
   E. take precautions to avoid a rush of blood away from the inmate's head

   4.____

5. It is not unknown that men have had themselves committed to prison in order to contact a person already in prison for the purpose of intimidation or conspiracy.
The one of the following situations to which the above statement is probably MOST relevant is the situation in which a

   5.____

A. first offender, who previously denied that he had any family, asks permission to attend his mother's funeral
B. second termer, previously docile, has become a serious disciplinary problem
C. hardened criminal, several times convicted for felonies, suddenly offers to give the warden information which he says is of great importance
D. first offender, a salesman in civilian life, asks repeatedly to be assigned to work at soap making
E. petty thief, many times convicted, repeatedly asks permission to take a correspondence course in radio mechanics

6. Of the following, the CHIEF justification for siversification of penal institutions is that

   A. the population of criminals includes many different types of persons
   B. each penal institution has its own peculiar problems
   C. penal institutions built at different times reflect different viewpoints
   D. not all prison sentences are definitely fixed by law
   E. the principles of penology are changing constantly

7. The officer supervising the admission of such an inmate should make a memorandum and see that such memorandum is delivered to the Warden or properly designated official immediately.
   The one of the following situations to which the above rule applies MOST directly is the admission of an inmate who

   A. is a recidivist
   B. has already been sentenced
   C. is over 50 years of age
   D. has previously attempted suicide
   E. is blind in one eye

8. Of the following, the CHIEF principle underlying the indeterminate sentence is that

   A. proper rehabilitation depends upon competent segregation of prisoners
   B. the maximum sentence for which a prisoner is committed should be clearly defined
   C. assignment of varying sentences for identical crimes tends to impair inmate morale
   D. punishment should fit the criminal rather than the crime
   E. youthful offenders are more easily rehabilitated if they are not placed behind prison bars

9. Of the following, the BEST reason for limiting the amount which any inmate can purchase from the prison commissary is to

   A. establish a positive incentive for good behavior
   B. maintain the commissary within practicable limits
   C. prevent gambling or attempts at bribery
   D. prevent smuggling of contraband
   E. avoid embezzlement of prison funds

10. Of the following, the CHIEF characteristic of a good probation system is

    A. uniform treatment for crimes of similar seriousness
    B. individualized study of each offender
    C. increased use of definite sentences

D. careful segregation of criminals while in the institution
E. participation by the parolees in policy determination

11. Of the following, the MOST accurate statement concerning self-committed drug addicts is that   11.____

    A. the inmate must be released by the original date set for discharge unless he requests longer confinement
    B. self-committed drug addicts earn good time at the rate of 5 days per month
    C. tentative discharge date is established as 60 days after commitment
    D. commitment must receive prior approval by the State Commissioner of Correction
    E. authorization of the Chief City Magistrate must be received by the Warden before release of the inmate

12. The one of the following MOST properly considered for transfer to Dannemora State Hospital is a   12.____

    A. mental defective who is psychoneurotic
    B. non-psychotic felon afflicted with tuberculosis
    C. mental defective who is not psychotic
    D. psychotic felon
    E. psychotic misdemeanant

13. Commitments to the City Reformatory are USUALLY made for a(n)   13.____

    A. definite period of time, depending upon the crime committed by the inmate
    B. indeterminate period, with payment of a fine permissible as an alternative
    C. definite period of time, with no alternative
    D. definite period of time, with payment of a fine permissible as an alternative for certain types of cases
    E. indeterminate period, depending upon the progress made by the inmate

14. Of the following, the LEAST accurate statement concerning bail procedure in the city Department of Correction is that the   14.____

    A. bail receipt is made out in duplicate
    B. bonds accepted for bail are enumerated in the bail receipt
    C. bail receipt indicates both the court and judge setting the bail
    D. original copy of the bail receipt is given to the surety
    E. cash or bonds accepted in bail are delivered to the City Treasurer's Office

15. Of the following, the securities LEAST acceptable in bail proceedings at city prisons are   15.____

    A. bonds of the Port of New York Authority
    B. bonds issued by the Home Owners Loan Corporation and guaranteed by the U.S. Government
    C. bonds of the State of New York
    D. bonds issued by the Federal Farm Mortgage Corporation and guaranteed by the U.S. Government
    E. U.S. Treasury Notes

16. Suppose that John Doe is sentenced for vagrancy on Thursday, September 1, to serve 30 days in the Workhouse. He receives full good time allowance.
Solely on the basis of the above information, his release date is MOST accurately fixed as September

    A. 23   B. 24   C. 25   D. 26   E. 27

17. Suppose that Richard Roe is sentenced on August 4 to serve 4 months in the Workhouse on a charge of petty larceny. He receives full good time allowance. Solely on the basis of the above information, his release date is MOST accurately fixed as

    A. December 23   B. January 3
    C. November 13   D. December 1
    E. November 17

18. According to the Rules and Regulations, a record shall be kept in a special book of all writs received.
The one of the following of which no record is generally made at an institution under the Department of Correction when a writ is received is the

    A. decision of the writ
    B. name of the judge allowing the writ
    C. name of the officer handling the writ
    D. date of commitment of the inmate mentioned in the writ
    E. provision of the Code of Criminal Procedure authorizing the writ

19. The Rules and Regulations specify the notation to be made when narcotics are found in a prison.
The one of the following NOT included in the specified notation is

    A. the type of narcotic found
    B. the names of witnesses
    C. the name of the institution
    D. the time and date of the incident
    E. whether the person on whom the narcotics were found was a visitor, employee, or inmate

20. According to the Rules and Regulations, *contraband* is BEST defined as any article

    A. which has been smuggled into the prison by an inmate
    B. which may be classified as a drug or alcoholic beverage
    C. detected by an Officer inspecting an inmate's cell
    D. which may be sold or exchanged by an inmate for personal favors by the uniformed staff or other inmates
    E. the presence of which within the prison may jeopardize its safety and good order

21. Sentences limited only by satisfactory proof of reformation should be substituted for those measured by mere lapse of time.
The above statement is BEST interpreted as an argument in favor of

    A. shorter sentences
    B. wider application of probation
    C. direct, as opposed to circumstantial evidence
    D. indeterminate sentences
    E. classification of inmates on basis of prison sentence

22. It must be recognized that, for some prisoners, punishment and deterrence rather than rehabilitation is the main purpose.
Of the following, the type of prisoner to whom this statement applies MOST accurately is the

    A. felon
    B. prisoner guilty of a crime against property
    C. juvenile delinquent
    D. prisoner gulity of a crime against the person
    E. short-term prisoner

23. If you segregated prisoners on every conceivable basis, you would eventually have only one man in each group. Of the following, the CHIEF implication of the above statement is that

    A. the individual rather than the group should be the essential basis to be considered in the segregation of prisoners
    B. the basis of segregation of prisoners has generally tended to be excessively wide in scope
    C. from the practical viewpoint the basis of segregation of prisoners must be restricted to a few important factors
    D. rehabilitation should be the aim of the segregation program
    E. every man in a penal institution should be treated as an individual and not as a member of a group

24. Assume that, as a correction supervisor, you are in charge of the Armory. A correction officer asks you what is meant by *leading* with respect to firearms.
You should inform him that *leading* means MOST nearly

    A. proper stance in markmanship drill
    B. accumulation of metal in the bore of the piece
    C. improving the balance of the piece
    D. erosion of the cocking mechanism
    E. adjustment of the range and windage devices

25. Instructionsim revolver marksmanshiposhould involve more than mere repetition of firing the revolver.
Of the following, the BEST justification for this statement is that

    A. mere instruction without practice in actually firing a revolver is valueless
    B. excellent marksmanship can best be obtained by frequent practice
    C. some men may require more practice and drill than others
    D. practice of wrong habits fails to improve marksmanship
    E. even competent marksmen require frequent practice

26. With reference to a revolver, *double action* refers MOST nearly to a revolver which

    A. fires and continues firing as long as the trigger is depressed
    B. ejects the empty cartridge, cocks the piece, and reloads when the trigger is squeezed
    C. ejects the empty cartridge and reloads in a single operation
    D. can be cocked only by pulling back the hammer
    E. can be cocked and fired simply by pulling the trigger

27. With reference to revolver marksmanship, *trajectory* means MOST nearly the

    A. speed and direction of the projectile when it leaves the revolver muzzle
    B. distance from the firing point to the target
    C. deflection or windage of the projectile
    D. path of the bullet from the muzzle to the target
    E. average height attained by the projectile in flight

28. Assume that, as a supervisor, you are instructing a group of newly appointed correction officers in the operation of the revolver.
    Of the following, it would be MOST accurate for you to instruct the group that the weight of a loaded .38 Colt official police revolver is _____ lb(s) _____ oz.

    A. 1; 14   B. 2; 1
    C. 2; 4   D. 2; 7
    E. 2; 10

29. Another device sometimes used is to pass a thread through the screen between visitor and inmate.
    The device described in the above statement is MOST likely to be used by an inmate who

    A. is planning to escape
    B. is a drug addict
    C. has stolen prison property which he wishes to dispose of
    D. wishes to pass an uncensored letter to the visitor
    E. is a chronic alcoholic

30. A legal hold against a defendent for further action of proper authorities.
    The above definition applies MOST accurately to

    A. a warrant   B. mandamus
    C. a subpoena   D. a writ of certiorari
    E. arraignment

31. Suppose that an inmate is awaiting trial at a prison. Before his attorney may visit the inmate, it is necessary that the attorney present a

    A. writ of habeas corpus from the appropriate court
    B. transcript demonstrating that a noticeoof appearance has been filed
    C. mandamus issued by the Supreme Court or Appellate Division
    D. writ of undertaking
    E. subpoena, properly filled out and sealed with the official seal

32. Of the following, the CHIEF function of the *Certificate of Reasonable Doubt* is to

    A. authorize a new trial on the grounds of erroneous conviction
    B. prevent transfer of an inmate to a State institution
    C. compel appearance of the defendant in court for a hearing on charges
    D. authorize acceptance of bail
    E. compel a person or body to do or refrain from doing a specific act

33. A court order directing a public official to perform a certain act which he has failed or refused to perform is called

    A. summary judgment
    B. mandamus
    C. default judgment
    D. declaratory judgment
    E. referendum

33.____

34. An order of a court, signed by a magistrate, judge, or clerk of the court, ordering that a defendant or material witness be held in custody.
This definition applies MOST accurately to

    A. indictment
    B. arraignment
    C. commitment
    D. subpoena
    E. bill of particulars

34.____

35. The one of the following crimes which is a felony in the State and for which imprisonment in a state institution is prescribed by law is

    A. assault in the third degree
    B. unlawful entry
    C. intoxicated driving (first offense)
    D. petty larceny (first offense)
    E. arson in the second degree

35.____

36. The Commissioner of Correction of the city shall have charge and custody of all the prisons and penitentiaries of the city.
Of the following, the primary body of law in which this provision appears is the

    A. State Constitution
    B. Criminal Procedure Law
    C. Penal Law
    D. City Administrative Code
    E. City Charter

36.____

37. According to the Administrative Code, the chief officer of any institution under the charge of the Commissioner of Correction shall report once in each week to the Commissioner. The one of the following which is NOT a category of information required by the Administrative Code to be included in this report is the

    A. quality and kind of labor performed in the institution
    B. discipline which has been maintained
    C. number of inmates available for release on parole
    D. number of inmates who have become sick
    E. number of persons who have been received, discharged, or transferred

37.____

38. Attempts to apply police training to prison personnel will have unsatisfactory results.
Of the following, the *most probable* cause of these poor results would be the

    A. difference in emphasis of the two fields of work
    B. failure to properly integrate classroom teaching with practical work
    C. poor quality of the instruction
    D. shortness of the training period generally used
    E. atmosphere in which the work is performed

38.____

39. A superior officer, investigating why an order had not been carried out, was told by the officers concerned that they had not realized that what the superior officer intended as an order.
    This incident illustrates *most directly* an order that was NOT

    A. concise
    B. possible of performance
    C. recognizable as an order
    D. reviewed after issuance of the order
    E. implicit

40. In explaining to a subordinate the importance of the tier officer's initial contact with a new admission, the superior officer should stress MOST the

    A. constructive influence this initial contact can have on the inmate's future adjustment to confinement
    B. desirability of getting the inmate to talk freely and without interruption
    C. harmful effect on the inmate's morale of a businesslike approach to the conduct of this initial interview
    D. value of this initial interview in impressing the inmate with the fact that violations of the rules will not be tolerated
    E. fear to be imbued in the inmate

KEY (CORRECT ANSWERS)

1.	D	11.	E	21.	D	31.	B
2.	E	12.	D	22.	E	32.	D
3.	B	13.	E	23.	C	33.	B
4.	C	14.	A	24.	B	34.	C
5.	D	15.	A	25.	D	35.	E
6.	A	16.	B	26.	E	36.	E
7.	D	17.	C	27.	D	37.	C
8.	D	18.	E	28.	C	38.	A
9.	C	19.	A	29.	B	39.	C
10.	B	20.	E	30.	A	40.	A

TEST 2

DIRECTIONS: Each question or incomplete statement is followed by several suggested answers or completions. Select the one that BEST answers the question or completes the statement. *PRINT THE LETTER OF THE CORRECT ANSWER IN THE SPACE AT THE RIGHT.*

1. If a correction officer is to perform his functions intelligently, he must be well acquainted with the literature concerning his field of work.
   The officer who is alert to publications in the field of penology should know that the author of the book *Stone Walls and Men* is (was)

    A. Austin H. MacCormick
    B. Thomas M. Osborne
    C. Lewis Lawes
    D. Leo Palmer
    E. Robert M. Lindner

    1.____

2. The PRISON WORLD is a journal devoted to the progressive administration of jails, prisons and reformatories.
   The competent officer should know that the organization which publishes the PRISON WORLD is the

    A. National Committe on Prisons
    B. American Prison Association
    C. American Institute of Criminology and Penology
    D. Osborne Association
    E. National Crime Prevention Institute

    2.____

3. The correction officer who had a professional interest in his work should know that the one of the following who is (was) BEST known for his writings in penology and criminology was

    A. Sanford Bates
    B. Norman L. Pressey
    C. Charles Skinner
    D. Carl J. Friedrick
    E. William P. McGowan

    3.____

4. Assume that, as a correction superior, you are supervising the preparation of a statistical report describing the inmate population in the institution to which you are assigned. You have available the following statistics: the number of first offenders, the number of inmates 40 years of age or over, and the number of inmates under 40 years of age.
   Of the following, the MOST accurate procedure for finding the fraction of all inmates who are first offenders is to

    A. divide the number of first offenders by the number of both inmates under 40 and inmates 40 or over who are first offenders
    B. find the fraction whose numerator is the difference between the total number of inmates and the number of first offenders and whose denominator is the total number of inmates
    C. add the ratio of first offenders to inmates under 40 and the ratio of first offenders to inmates 40 or over
    D. divide the number of first offenders by the sum of inmates under 40 and inmates 40 or over
    E. divide twice the number of first offenders by the total of all inmates

    4.____

2 (#2)

5. Suppose that the average cost of feeding inmates in your institution during the month of June is 2 cents a day greater than the average cost during the month of April. Then, of the following, the MOST accurate statement is that

    A. the increase in total cost of feeding inmates from April to June is 2 cents times the average number of inmates during April
    B. the increase in total cost of feeding inmates from April to June is 2 cents times the average number of inmates during June
    C. comparison of the average cost of feeding a single inmate during June and during April is impossible without further information concerning the number of inmates involved
    D. the total cost per inmate for the month of June exceeds the total cost per inmate for the month of April by an amount equal to 60 times the increase in the number of inmates from April to June
    E. the total cost per inmate for the month of June is 60 cents greater than the total cost per inmate for the month of April, regardless of the number of inmates

5.___

6. Assume that the average number of daily admissions during the first half of 2003 to the institution to which you are assigned as a supervisor is less that the average number of daily admissions during all of 2002.
Then, of the following, the MOST accurate statement is that if the

    A. average number of daily admissions for all of 2003 is to equal the average number of daily admissions for 2002, the total admissions for the second half of 2003 must exceed the total admissions for all of 2002
    B. total admissions for 2002 is to exceed the total admissions for all of 2003, the total admissions for the second half of 2003 must exceed the total admissions for the second half of 2002
    C. total admissions for all of 2003 is to exceed the total number of admissions for 2002, the average number of daily admissions for the second half of 2003 must be greater than the average number of daily admissions for all of 2002
    D. average daily admissions for 2002 is to be less than the average daily admissions for all of 2003, the average daily admissions for the second half of 2002 must be greater than the average daily admissions for the second half of 2003
    E. total admissions for the second half of 2003 exceeds the total admissions for the corresponding period in 2002, the average daily admissions for 2003 will exceed the average daily admissions for 2002

6.___

7. To understand the problem of narcotic drug addiction, one must realize that, when a person has used an opiate for a considerable length of time, a change takes place in his internal economy, so that he becomes physically dependent on the drug. The result of this change is that if the dosage is suddenly discontinued he becomes physically ill. Of the following, the drug to which the above statement applies MOST directly is

    A. cocaine   B. peyote
    C. marijuana   D. heroin
    E. alcohol

7.___

8. The newly appointed correction officer reported to his superior that an inmate under his supervision seemed very quiet and highly withdrawn. The inmate would sit motionless, apparently daydreaming, for hours at a time. The correction officer said, however, that he decided to ignore this inmate in favor of observing more closely the aggressive and boisterous inmates.
   As a superior, you should realize that the correction officer's action was *unwise* CHIEFLY because

   A. no one inmate should receive more attention than any other
   B. aggressive inmates are more likely to be disciplinary problems than withdrawn inmates
   C. an inmate may be withdrawn one day and boisterous the next day
   D. the unusually aggressive person is more difficult to detect than the withdrawn person
   E. the unusually quiet inmate may have serious mental problems

8.____

9. Of the following, the MOST accurate statement concerning feeblemindedness is that

   A. the distinction between the feebleminded and normal is so sharp that persons with borderline intelligence are rarely found
   B. a mentally retarded person, by definition, is considered a moral delinquent
   C. a determination of feeblemindedness on the basis of psychological test score should be corroborated by evidence of lack of social adjustment
   D. the person who is feebleminded is likely to be above average in physical strength
   E. although feebleminded persons cannot generally be recognized by facial characteristics, most morons can be recognized in this manner

9.____

10. The correction supervisor will soon learn to recognize whether an inmate is a constitutional psychopath.
    Of the following, the MOST accurate statement concerning a constitutional psychopath is that he

    A. is usually psychotic or insane
    B. is subject to violent hallucinations and delusions
    C. is likely to be withdrawn and morose
    D. is chronically in conflict with social laws and customs
    E. his illness is due to organic brain lesion

10.____

11. Of the following, the BEST justification for encouraging a correction officer to ask questions about the proper performance of his duties is that

    A. the number of questions asked is an excellent index of efficiency on the job
    B. learning by doing is an effective training principle
    C. confusion on even minor points may have serious consequences
    D. the question and answer method is especially efficient when a large number of correction officers must be trained
    E. the correction officer who asks questions demonstrates a lack of general orientation to the job

11.____

12. Inspections of the uniformed force should be made by the correction superior at irregular rather than regular intervals CHIEFLY because

    A. excessive preoccupation with routine detail is likely to stifle initiative on the part of the correction superior
    B. unexpected inspections encourage a uniformly high level of performance
    C. conditions are likely to change rapidly without previous warning
    D. an unexpected inspection may give an inaccurate picture of work performance
    E. avoidance of a precise inspection schedule affords the correction superior adequate opportunity to handle special matters

13. A personal conference is generally a more desirable procedure for reprimanding a correction officer than a public reprimand CHIEFLY because a

    A. private reprimand makes a deeper impression on the individual
    B. public reprimand is more suitable for a group of two or three persons than for a single individual
    C. public reprimand may impair the morale of the individual
    D. private reprimand can be accomplished more quickly and saves the time of both the supervisor and the correction officer
    E. reprimand, if it is to be effective, must be impartial and impersonal

14. Assume that, as a superior, you are giving a correction officer under your supervision instructions to perform a rather complex assignment.
    Of the following, the BEST procedure to follow in order to insure that he understands the instructions adequately is to

    A. have him repeat the instructions word for word
    B. invite him to ask questions if he has any doubts
    C. check the progress of his work at the first opportunity
    D. question him briefly concerning the chief aspects of the assignment
    E. be certain to check his performance as soon as he has completed the job

15. Suppose that, as a superior, you observe that a newly appointed correction officer under your supervision appears to be performing a specific assignment improperly. Of the following, the BEST reason for asking him to repeat the instructions he received is that

    A. efficient correction officers rarely need specific or detailed instructions
    B. it is often easier to review instructions than to repeat them
    C. the correction officer obviously deserves a reprimand
    D. inefficiency on the part of the uniformed force may have serious consequences
    E. instructions are sometimes misunderstood even by competent subordinates

16. Assume that, as a correction supervisor, you are assigned to conduct a refresher training course for correction officers. Of the following, the BEST reason for employing group discussion procedures rather than routine lecture methods is that

    A. learning is more efficient when men participate actively in the process
    B. the scope of a training course can be laid out more precisely when one person is held responsible for the course
    C. the more experienced the men, the more likely they can benefit from a lecture course

D. less time need be devoted to a course which has a well defined purpose
E. a greater number of topics can be covered in a course when several people participate

17. Assume that, as a correction superior, you are frequently called upon to submit reports on special problems to the Warden.
Of the following, the LEAST valid statement of a principle to be followed in the preparation of good reports is that

    A. the report should present all the evidence upon which conclusions are based
    B. independent ideas should be discussed in separate paragraphs
    C. paragraphs should all be about equal in length
    D. detailed statistical tables should be relegated to the appendix
    E. If the report is lengthy, a summary or list of recommendations should be given at the beginning of the report

17.____

18. Good discipline and secure custody may not be the MOST important functions of a jail, but from the practical viewpoint it is obviously impossible to carry out the purposes of an institution except on a foundation of sound discipline.
Of the following, the CHIEF implication of the above statement is that

    A. good discipline is a means to an end rather than an objective in itself
    B. when discipline is good, the chief objective of a prison has been attained
    C. practically speaking, certain functions of a jail are obviously impossible
    D. discipline is the sound foundation upon which secure custody can be maintained
    E. good discipline and secure custody are objectives rather than functions of a jail

18.____

19. The competent superior will be friendly with the correction officers under his supervision but will avoid close familiarity.
Of the following, the BEST justification for this statement is that

    A. familiarity with the correction officers may reveal lack of competence on the part of the superior
    B. a superior can deal more competently with correction officers when he is not aware of their personal problems
    C. a friendly attitude on the part of the superior towards a correction officer is likely to create suspicion on the part of the correction officer
    D. familiarity between a superior and a correction officer creates an appearance of special privileges
    E. the superior's attitude toward correction officers need not be the same as his attitude toward the inmates

19.____

20. Responsibility for the general enforcement of discipline and the administration of punishment for infractions should be invested in one officer, usually the warden himself or one of his deputies.
Of the following, the BEST justification for this statement is that

    A. discipline should be prompt if it is to be effective
    B. punishment should usually be administered by the person in closest relationship to the offender
    C. a formalized and inflexible system of punishment is likely to defeat itself

20.____

D. a system of discipline and punishments should be uniform, so far as possible
E. discipline is likely to be ineffective unless offenses and punishments are known to all beforehand

21. Adequate training of uniformed personnel can facilitate the rehabilitation program.
Of the following, the BEST justification for this statement is that

   A. the uniformed personnel, in practice, includes the entire custodial force, from warden to correction officer
   B. facility in training is a necessary requisite for the competent supervision of uniformed personnel
   C. the rehabilitation program of a penal institution is essentially formalized in training aspects
   D. correction officers should be educated to detect devices employed by inmates to outwit the uniformed force
   E. the attitudes and conduct of the correction officers determine, in large part, the correctional value of a penal institution

22. Suppose that you are a correction supervisor. Of the following, the BEST justification for acquainting yourself with the background and capabilities of each correction officer under your supervision is that

   A. the work of a correction officer is of a highly important nature and demands a trustworthy person of unblemished background
   B. some correction officers may seek advice on purely personal matters
   C. nearly all men are equipped with the basic ability to do the same job equally well
   D. superior background shortly becomes evident in superior work quality, regardless of assignment
   E. some correction officers are better fitted for certain assignments than others on the basis of background

23. The competent correction superior will attempt to develop respect rather than fear on the part of the men under his supervision.
Of the following, the CHIEF justification for this statement is that

   A. experience has demonstrated that negative incentives are more effective than positive incentives
   B. respect is based on the individual and fear is based on the organization as a whole
   C. respect on the part of the men is generally easier to develop than fear of penalty
   D. men who respect a supervisor are likely to give more than the minimum required performance
   E. respect of superiors is a general incentive whereas fear is a specific incentive

24. The one of the following statements which is MOST accurate is that, at the time of accepting bail, an affidavit is signed by the

   A. surety which relinquishes any claim to the money or bonds placed as bail
   B. inmate which establishes his claim to the money or bonds placed as bail
   C. surety which indicates what remuneration he has received or has been promised for furnishing the bail

D. Warden or his duly appointed representative which establishes that the surety's equity is sufficient to cover the cash or property offered as bail
E. surety and the inmate which establishes the sufficiency of the equity and their right to offer such equity for purposes of bail

25. Of the following, the type of offense committed by an inmate for which indictment and subsequent conviction by a court is a procedure MORE appropriate than routine institutional punishment is

    A. insolence to a correction officer
    B. refusal to work
    C. fighting with another inmate
    D. escape from lawful custody
    E. intentional damage to prison property

26. Assume that a warrant for an inmate has been received by mail from the Police Department.
    The one of the following which describes LEAST accurately an action taken under these circumstances is that

    A. receipt of the warrant is acknowledged immediately
    B. immediately upon receipt of the warrant, the Police Department is notified of the date of release of the prisoner
    C. when the Police Department is notified of the date of release of the prisoner, acknowledgment of receipt of this information is requested
    D. on the inmate's release date, the warrant is returned to the arresting officer
    E. the inmate is turned over to the arresting officer on the morning of the inmate's discharge

27. Assume that you are a superior. A newly appointed correction officer under your supervision asks you why the Rules and Regulations forbid accepting gifts even when the gifts are inexpenisve and no special favor has been shown the inmate.
    Of the following, the BEST answer for you to give is that

    A. proper rehabilitation of the inmate offering the gift will be impossible if the gift is accepted
    B. the express permission of the Warden or his Deputy must be obtained beforehand
    C. accepting even inexpensive gifts for routine performance of duties may damage the reputation of the institution
    D. the inmate who offers gifts is usually engaged in some kind of illegal activity in the prison
    E. the fact that a gift has been offered proves that special favors have been given

28. Of the following, the statement concerning the administration of prison discipline which is generally LEAST accurate is that

    A. treatment of inmates by custodial employees should be consistent
    B. inmates should be made aware of the rules and regulations
    C. concessions should not be made to inmates who are demonstrating or striking against the administration
    D. no inmate should be deprived of privileges available to other inmates
    E. no cash money should be allowed in the possession of inmates under any circumstances

8 (#2)

29. Of the following, the LEAST accurate statement concerning the procedure employed for the collection of cash fines at an institution under the Department of Correction is that

   A. cash only may be accepted in payment of a fine
   B. partial payment of a fine may be accepted only if specifically states in the commitment
   C. serial numbers must be listed of all bills higher than $1 in denomination accepted in payment of fines
   D. after collection of the fine, the procedure for discharging the inmate is similar to that pursued at the expiration of his sentence
   E. on commitment for a definite period of time plus a fine, a fine can be accepted only after expiration of the definite period

30. To be an incentive, time off for good behavior must not be a routine award.
Of the following, the CHIEF implication of the above statement is that

   A. time off for good behavior is rarely an incentive in itself
   B. awards should be routinely administered if they are to be free of favoritism as incentives
   C. care should be exercised by the custodial force in recommending time for good behavior
   D. nearly all persons should be allowed to earn time off for good behavior
   E. determination of time off for good behavior should not be relegated to custodial forces

31. Of the following, the MOST accurate statement concerning penitentiary definite sentences is that the inmate

   A. receives no credit for time awaiting trial
   B. must serve three months in the penitentiary, exclusive of jail time, before he may receive credit for good time
   C. is allowed by law five days per month commutation for good behavior
   D. receives credit for time elapsed from the day of sentence to the day he is received at the penitentiary
   E. is allowed by law two days per month commutation for good behavior

32. In volume, 90 percent of the sentences in the city are to jail and generally for short terms such as 5, 10 or 30 days. Only about 1/4 of the jail cases are first offenders.
Of the following, the CHIEF implication of the above statement for the work of the Department of Correction is that

   A. more careful screening of prisoners is necessary
   B. short sentences are a causal factor leading to recidivism
   C. time available for rehabilitation is inadequate for most inmates
   D. persons sentenced for short terms are generally first offenders
   E. more careful segregation of prisoners is desirable

33. Some people attribute crime to lack of schooling, bad environment, or undesirable associations; others insist that its specific cause is the pistol, liquor, or the automobile. One cannot choose any one specific factor at random and conclude that it was the sole cause of a crime. Of the following, the CHIEF implication of the above statement is that

A. factors associated with crime are usually specific rather than random
B. crimes may usually be attributed to a combination of factors
C. general factors lead to crime more usually than specific factors
D. a general factor such as lack of schooling will not usually produce a crime unless there is a specific cause
E. whereas specific factors cannot be considered the sole cause of a crime, a criminal's background may be

34. Of the following, the most valid argument AGAINST the indeterminate sentence is that   34.____

    A. the possibility of early release is a poor incentive to inmates
    B. good behavior in a prison is sometimes a conscious deception
    C. the time required for rehabilitation is often not the same for different inmates
    D. it is economical for the State to release a prisoner after a reasonable degree of rehabilitation is achieved
    E. the prisoner who believes he received fair treatment is less likely to be a recidivist

35. Of the following, the MOST accurate statement concerning the cottage group system is that it   35.____

    A. provides different treatment for separate groups of prisoners
    B. has been used most frequently with adult males
    C. allows all prisoners almost unlimited freedom with complete responsibility
    D. is designed especially for the high grade feebleminded
    E. emphasizes education rather than labor for illiterates

36. Any prisoner who is mentally and physically sound, regardless of his past, is not entirely beyond rehabilitation.   36.____
    Of the following, the MOST valid inference on the basis of the above statement is that

    A. an important cause of crime may be irremediable
    B. the possibility of rehabilitating men with previous criminal records is remote
    C. rehabilitation usually requires treatment for both mental and physical disabilities
    D. prisoners who are mentally and physically sound usually do not require rehabilitation
    E. the problem of rehabilitation must be considered apart from mental status and past record

37. We have been able to gather together, in penal institutions, groups of individuals who are more like themselves than they are like the members of any other group.   37.____
    Of the following, the CHIEF advantage of the procedure described in the above statement is that

    A. specialized procedures are possible
    B. stricter discipline can be maintained
    C. social training and adjustment are possible
    D. parole procedures can be established
    E. assignment to work is possible for all inmates

38. Of the following, the type of prisoner MOST properly sent to a farm colony or camp is a

   A. feebleminded youth, aged 18
   B. man, aged 55, arrested for the fourth time for vagrancy
   C. first offender, aged 22, apprehended after escape from custody
   D. youth, aged 23, sentenced for 20 years for a serious felony
   E. first offender, aged 25, who seems to be suffering a serious mental disturbance

39. Of the following, the prisoner who would be LEAST likely to attempt to escape is probably the

   A. young prisoner who has no family ties
   B. married prisoner who is uncertain and worried about the health of his wife
   C. mature prisoner who has a long criminal record
   D. first offender who has not yet been committed but expects a short term
   E. first offender who has warrants filed against him from other jurisdictions

40. The ideally disciplined group, with standards of conduct uniformly high, would never need to be punished or rewarded.
   Of the following, the BEST justification for this statement is that

   A. punishment and reward are relatively ineffective as disciplinary measures
   B. a group must already be well disciplined if punishment is to affect standards of conduct
   C. in a well disciplined group each man acts to the best of his ability
   D. only in the ideal are discipline and standards conduct synonomous terms
   E. wise application of punishment and rewards will produce an ideally disciplined group

---

KEY (CORRECT ANSWERS)

1.	E	11.	C	21.	E	31.	B
2.	B	12.	B	22.	E	32.	C
3.	A	13.	C	23.	D	33.	B
4.	D	14.	D	24.	C	34.	B
5.	E	15.	E	25.	D	35.	A
6.	C	16.	A	26.	B	36.	A
7.	D	17.	C	27.	C	37.	A
8.	E	18.	A	28.	D	38.	B
9.	C	19.	D	29.	E	39.	D
10.	D	20.	D	30.	C	40.	C

EXAMINATION SECTION
TEST 1

DIRECTIONS: Each question or incomplete statement is followed by several suggested answers or completions. Select the one that BEST answers the question or completes the statement. *PRINT THE LETTER OF THE CORRECT ANSWER IN THE SPACE AT THE RIGHT.*

1. Of the following, the MOST serious problem to be faced in the proper supervision of new correction officers is that, for the most part, these officers

    A. are afraid to face up to the responsibilities of their position
    B. are over-confident and have a *know-it-all* attitude
    C. have accepted this employment only as a stopgap until they find other work
    D. have had no extensive formal training in this field of work

2. An employee's performance should be evaluated quarterly during the probationary period, and at least once a year after the probationary period. Of the following, the CHIEF justification for the less frequent formal evaluation of employee performance after the probationary period is that

    A. over-supervision of experienced employees is unnecessary and undesirable and may create resentment on the part of the employee
    B. the employee has already proven himself satisfactory by passing his probationary period
    C. the older employee reacts more quickly and responsively to supervision
    D. the supervisor has already achieved a considerable degree of familiarity with the employee's capabilities, performance and need for further training

3. It has been suggested that the in-service training of employees in the correctional field be continued from the time of their employment until the time of their leaving the department. Of the following, the CHIEF justification for such a continuous program of in-service training is that

    A. a person's capacity for learning increases with age
    B. because of a natural tendency to forget what one has learned and not put into practice, training must be repeated at regular intervals
    C. employees usually are capable of further development on the job during the entire period of their employment
    D. for learning to be effective, successive stages in the learning process must be correlated and coordinated

4. Of the following, the CHIEF advantage of rotating the qualified staff of a correctional institution among the various job assignments is the

    A. development of versatility in staff members
    B. elimination of jealousy among employees
    C. establishment of bases upon which to formulate work norms
    D. lessening of the undesirable trend toward increasing specialization

19

5. It has been stated that the key to successful application of the majority of standards that have been set for an adult correctional institution is the proper organization, selection, training, and assignment of the staff. Of the following, the CHIEF justification for this statement is that

   A. proper selection, training, organization, and assignment of staff are often a neglected phase of institutional management
   B. proper staffing is the most complex aspect of correctional institution management
   C. staff selection, training, organization, and assignment is a continuous process
   D. the staff is the medium through which these standards must be implemented

6. Of the following, the MOST important reason why supervisors should give careful consideration to the techniques they utilize for assignment of employees to specific jobs is that

   A. an opportunity is thus offered the supervisor for periodic evaluation of the qualifications and work performance of all employees
   B. efficiency of employees is dependent in part on the techniques used by supervisory officers for selection of employees for assignments
   C. requests of employees for change in work assignments may indicate dissatisfaction with present conditions
   D. standardized techniques for the selection of employees for specific job assignments have not yet been developed

7. In the selection and appointment process for correction officers, particular care is taken to screen out the neurotic and unstable. Suppose, however, that in spite of this, as a result of your observations during the probationary period you are convinced that a new officer appointed to your command has a neurotic and unstable personality. Of the following, the BEST action for you to take as supervisor is to

   A. give restricted assignment and close supervision to this officer unless the need for more drastic action is indicated at a later date
   B. help the employee to correct this undesirable trait by giving proper and continuous training
   C. recommend that the employee be dropped at the end of the probationary period
   D. refer the employee for appropriate medical care

8. Attempts to apply police training to prison personnel will have unsatisfactory results. Of the following, the MOST probable cause of these poor results would be the

   A. difference in emphasis of the two fields of work
   B. failure to properly integrate classroom teaching with practical work
   C. poor quality of the instruction
   D. shortness of the training period generally used

9. Of the following, the LEAST desirable use of a new officer's probationary period by the supervisor is to

   A. carefully check and evaluate performance of work assigned
   B. instruct the officer in the proper performance of assigned duties
   C. observe whether the officer is capable of performing the duties of the job efficiently
   D. train the officer for promotion to the next higher rank

10. The statement has been made that correction officers have a tendency to get into a rut. If this statement is valid, the one of the following actions by an officer which BEST illustrates this tendency is

    A. continuing in the same assignment for several years without being motivated to ask for a change in assignment
    B. performing an act of alertness or heroism after the incident which might have been prevented by such act has already been precipitated
    C. releasing an inmate after partial identification, taking for granted that it must be the correct inmate
    D. using the standard, approved methods of conducting their searches for contraband instead of trying to devise more ingenious and novel methods

10._____

11. A superior, investigating why an order had not been carried out, was told by the officers concerned that they had not realized that what the superior had told them was intended as an order. This incident illustrates MOST directly an order that was not

    A. concise
    B. possible of performance
    C. recognizable as an order
    D. reviewed after issuance of the order

11._____

12. In explaining to a subordinate the importance of the tier officer's initial contact with a new admission, the superior should stress MOST the

    A. constructive influence this initial contact can have on the inmate's future adjustment to confinement
    B. desirability of getting the inmate to talk freely and without interruption
    C. harmful effect on the inmate's morale of a businesslike approach in the conduct of this initial interview
    D. value of this initial interview in impressing the inmate with the fact that violations of the rules will not be tolerated

12._____

13. In explaining to a group of new officers the reasons why their position is so important in the operations of the Department, the supervisor should emphasize MOST the fact that

    A. the inmate's attitude to the officer is basically a hostile one
    B. the largest number of uniformed personnel is in the rank of correction officer
    C. the officer represents the most frequent, direct contact of the Department with the inmate
    D. this is the rank from which the administrative positions in the Department will be filled

13._____

14. Each job assignment of personnel in the institution should be carefully described in writing, setting forth the duties, responsibilities, and special requirements of the particular job assignment. Of the following, the CHIEF advantage of this procedure is that

    A. a change in administration or supervision will not interfere with the orderly running of the institution
    B. defects in administrative organization will become apparent

14._____

C. employees will have a ready means of knowing what is expected of them in their particular assignments
D. it will be possible to transfer employees more freely from one job assignment to another

15. If, as supervisor, you find that there occur a considerable number of minor, apparently unintentional infractions of rules by inmates on one officer's post, the BEST action of the following for you to take FIRST would be to

    A. determine if the inmates on this post have a clear understanding of the rules and what constitutes violation of the rules
    B. find out the basic causes of inmate dissatisfaction on this post and correct them
    C. give this officer additional training in proper techniques for maintaining stricter discipline on the post
    D. investigate whether it would be advisable to assign a more competent officer to this post

15.___

16. Suppose you learn that an officer under your command intends to file an official complaint against an inmate for committing an infraction of the institution's rules.
Of the following, the BEST action for you to take as captain is to

    A. advise the officer that the filing of official complaints should be reserved for the most serious infractions only
    B. determine if the infraction is serious enough to warrant an official complaint
    C. make an inspection to determine whether discipline on the post is otherwise satisfactory
    D. support the officer in the interest of maintaining institution discipline and morale

16.___

17. Suppose it comes to your attention that an officer under your supervision does not give prompt consideration to all complaints and requests of inmates. Of the following, the BEST action for you to take is to

    A. discuss with the officer the harmful effect such action can have on inmate morale
    B. explain to the officer that action on complaints must be differentiated from action on requests
    C. order the officer to comply with all inmate complaints and requests promptly
    D. warn the officer and give closer supervision as something serious might result from this method of work

17.___

18. In explaining to a correction officer why an unvaried routine in the conduct of tier post inspections is not desirable, a supervisor should stress MOST the fact that

    A. a method of work that may be entirely acceptable in one situation generally proves to be unacceptable when transferred without modification to a different work situation
    B. inmates seeking to violate the institution's rules make a study of the officer's habits so that they can time their activities to forestall detection
    C. it is important to have a clear understanding of the purposes of the tier post inspection in order to be able to carry it out efficiently and intelligently
    D. the discovery of contraband is not the sole purpose of a tier post inspection

18.___

19. A superior instructed subordinates in the meaning of parole, the conditions under which it is granted, and in the rules and practices of parole supervision. The superior's action was

    A. *necessary and desirable;* the entire prison staff should have an understanding of parole if the indoctrination and orientation of the inmates with respect to parole is to be well done
    B. *unnecessary and undesirable;* only occasionally does a member of the superior's staff have any responsibilities directly connected with the parole function
    C. *necessary and desirable; while* the staff generally has no concern with parole matters and problems, they should have a well-rounded background which includes a knowledge of related agencies
    D. *unnecessary and undesirable;* the parole function is the responsibility of another agency

20. Of the following, the LEAST important rule for a supervisor to stress when instructing an officer in the fundamentals of making a count of prisoners is:

    A. Count each tier of a cell block separately and make a temporary note of the count for each tier
    B. Do not speak to prisoners or to other personnel when making a count
    C. See flesh or movement or hear prisoners speak before recording them as counted
    D. Speak the number out loud as you count each inmate so that you can actually be heard making the count

21. A supervisor instructed a group of new officers that before beginning their tier count when coming on duty, they should get the off-going officer's last count and use this as a check when making their count. The supervisor's instructions were

    A. *good,* because a new officer should receive assistance from an experienced officer
    B. *poor,* because errors in the previous count may be unconsciously duplicated
    C. *good,* because both counts must agree
    D. *poor,* because the oncoming officer is not in any way responsible for the off-going officer's count

22. A superior instructed subordinates that, at all times, the tier officer going off duty was to notify the oncoming officer of any inmate who should be particularly watched. The superior's instructions were

    A. *good,* because the on-coming officer will not be surprised if any inmate behaves strangely
    B. *poor,* because alertness and initiative on the part of the on-coming officer may be reduced
    C. *good,* because the on-coming officer will benefit from the experiences and observation of the off-going officer
    D. *poor,* because all inmates should be given careful and close custody and supervision

23. Of the following, the technique that is likely to contribute MOST to the successful control of suicides in a correction command is for the supervisor to

    A. explain to subordinates some of the most common methods by which inmates commit suicide
    B. keep subordinates informed of the latest statistics on suicides in the Department's institutions as a sobering reminder that constant attention to duty is required
    C. stress to subordinates repeatedly the serious effect on the institution of a successful suicide
    D. train subordinates in spotting the inmates who may be potential suicides

24. A supervisor stated to a group of newly appointed correction officers: *I cannot emphasize to you too much the importance of frequent patrol of your post.* The supervisor MOST probably placed such great emphasis on the importance of frequent patrol because

    A. many captains neglect to develop in their subordinates a proper understanding of and technique for the post patrol
    B. most officers do not patrol often enough
    C. patrol is the best way for an officer to keep in touch with what is happening on his post
    D. patrol is the best way of developing regular habits of work in a correction officer

25. Suppose that two experienced officers assigned to a tier post report to you that they suspect there is contraband hidden on the post but that they have been unable to locate it in spite of several searches. As supervisor, the BEST thing for you to do at this time is to

    A. advise the officers to continue to be on the alert and to make several more searches at unexpected times
    B. explain to the officers that it is pointless to persist in these suspicions when they have not been substantiated by the facts
    C. organize and supervise a special search of the tier with a selected group of officers
    D. review the techniques employed by the officers in conducting these searches and point out why they are faulty

26. A cautious and observant officer seldom becomes involved in litigation initiated by an inmate who is injured during confinement on a tier. This statement is MOST probably based on the principle that such an officer will

    A. avoid and prevent situations which might cause injury to an inmate
    B. avoid any and all disputes with inmates
    C. be able to persuade the inmate that litigation is not justified
    D. make sure that any injury to an inmate is the result of the inmate's own negligence

27. Of the following, the factor that contributes MOST to making the problem of custodial supervision in a prison so difficult is the

    A. few troublesome inmates who do not adjust
    B. lack of adequate space and facilities
    C. shortage of staff
    D. unnatural environment of a prison

28. A supervisor is summoned by a correction officer to the cell of a newly committed inmate who has been taken suddenly ill. After observing the inmate, the supervisor thinks that the inmate's condition is due to nervous excitement resulting from commitment to the institution. The supervisor should

    A. speak quietly to the inmate until a normal condition is restored
    B. give the inmate a mild sedative
    C. make the inmate comfortable and instruct the officer to keep a close watch
    D. secure medical assistance for the inmate

29. Of the following, the type of inmate in whom arrest and confinement are likely to cause the GREATEST emotional shock is the

    A. adolescent offender
    B. adult of established family in the community
    C. mental defective
    D. recidivist who was confident of not getting caught

30. The maintenance of the personal cleanliness of inmates through the medium of regular bathing assumes added importance in a prison MAINLY because

    A. it is another procedure by which the possession of contraband by inmates can often be discovered
    B. most inmates have not developed proper habits of cleanliness
    C. personal body cleanliness is important in all individuals, including prison inmates
    D. the confining nature of institutional life necessarily brings inmates into close daily contact with each other

31. From the standpoint of custody, the first concern of the correction officer in the court pen should be to lock the inmate in the pen as soon as possible. Of the following, the CHIEF justification for this statement is the fact that the officer

    A. can more easily take an accurate count of inmates confined in the pen
    B. can then give undivided attention to other important duties
    C. does not know how soon the inmate will have to be produced in court again
    D. may be the only obstacle between the inmate and escape

32. In the event that an officer discovers an attempted suicide by an inmate, the FIRST thing the officer should do is

    A. administer first aid
    B. gather all the evidence
    C. go to summon the institution physician
    D. notify the head of the institution

33. When an inmate commits a serious infraction of discipline, the supervisor is required to investigate the incident as soon as practicable, but not later than the same day. Of the following, the CHIEF justification for such prompt investigation is that

    A. an investigation delayed is usually forgotten
    B. memory of the incident will be more accurate in the minds of participants and witnesses

C. the inmate will be impressed with the seriousness of the offense
D. the various participants and witnesses concerned in the incident will have less opportunity to prepare false versions of what actually happened

34. An officer should NOT use force toward an inmate for the purpose of

   A. compelling obedience to an order
   B. curbing a riot
   C. protecting the inmate's life
   D. self-defense

35. Cell location is an important factor in the custody and security of inmates who may be potential suicides PRIMARILY because

   A. cell location has an important effect on the morale of inmates
   B. in some cells it is easier to conceal contraband
   C. the ease of committing suicide varies from cell to cell
   D. the officer can keep certain cells under close observation more easily

36. Familiarity with the statistical information about suicides and attempted suicides in the institutions of the Department is of value to supervisors MAINLY because such information

   A. can assist the supervisor in personally detecting and preventing a greater number of suicides
   B. can be used as a basis of comparison with what is happening on the correction command
   C. can be used as an aid in training subordinates in the detection and prevention of suicides
   D. gives the supervisor a broader understanding of the success of the Department in carrying out its objectives

37. In the institutions of the Department, special security procedures are observed with an inmate sentenced to death or to a long term in a state prison. Such special procedures are advisable MAINLY because the

   A. Department is only temporarily responsible for someone who is actually a prisoner of the State
   B. inmate's friends and accomplices on the outside may attempt to free the inmate by force
   C. isolation of such inmate from the rest of the prison population is not practicable
   D. severity of the sentence may impel such inmate to commit some desperate act

38. An advantage of frequent special tier searches for contraband, although often no contraband may be discovered in such searches, is that

   A. inmates are placed on notice that contraband will not be tolerated in the institution
   B. negligence on the part of the tier officer with respect to contraband control does not have serious results
   C. officers are given training in military discipline
   D. responsibility for contraband control on the post is shared equally by superior and subordinate

39. When assigned to duty in a large mess hall during inmate mess, it is important for officers to station themselves in such a way that they can see and be seen by their superior at all times. This statement is justified MAINLY because the

    A. inmates will not attempt to create any disturbance when they see that the officers and their superior are in ready communication with each other
    B. officers will be able to show their superior that they are performing their jobs properly
    C. officers will be able to tell if the superior has left the mess hall
    D. superior, who may be far away from the officers, might suddenly find it necessary to transmit an order to them quickly by means of a signal

40. The sole value of the maintenance of proper sanitation procedures on a tier post is the protection of the health of the inmates and of the prison personnel. This statement is

    A. *correct,* because the health of inmates and personnel must be protected at all times, in the interest of proper institutional administration
    B. *incorrect,* because proper post sanitation also has other values, such as morale building
    C. *correct,* because the poor physical and moral condition of many inmates creates an undue amount of sanitation problems
    D. *incorrect,* because there has been no positive evidence that cleanliness on a tier post actually affects health

41. The primary function of the prison is the safekeeping of the prisoners committed to the prison. This statement is

    A. *invalid,* because it ignores the latest concepts in correctional work, which emphasize the rehabilitative potentialities of imprisonment
    B. *valid,* because statistics on recidivism show that it is the only function capable of realization
    C. *invalid,* because the prison has several functions, each of which is greatly important
    D. *valid,* because the prison is legally responsible for the safe custody of the prisoners committed by the courts until the expiration of their sentences

42. In its inmate treatment program, a correctional institution should operate on the philosophy that well-adjusted people do more than merely sleep, eat, and work. Of the following, the MOST valid inference based on this statement is that an additional important function of the correctional institution is to

    A. give inmates an insight into the problems and conflicts of well-adjusted people
    B. prepare inmates for employment in useful work
    C. train inmates in proper use of leisure time
    D. train inmates to strike a proper balance between work and rest

43. All the processes in a correctional institution should be directed toward educating the individual for successful community living. Of the following, the factor that contributes MOST to making this task a difficult one is the

    A. absence of a clear definition as to what constitutes successful community living
    B. conflict of interest between community and institution

C. competitive nature of modern day community life
D. need to change unacceptable behavior patterns into patterns acceptable to the community

44. It has been recommended that the work week of inmates employed in a program of prison industries be the same as the work week for similar employment in private industry. From the standpoint of the major objectives of a prison industries program, the adoption of this recommendation is desirable MAINLY because

   A. it will make possible the inclusion of a wider variety of employments in the prison industries program
   B. it will tend to make the deterrent objective of imprisonment more effective
   C. the prison industries will then be more profitable to operate since production will be greater
   D. the rehabilitative process will be aided if conditions of work approach those in real life

45. The work assignment of inmates should be based on other factors in addition to their request for particular assignments. Of the following, the LEAST important reason for this is that the inmates

   A. may have questionable motives for requesting particular assignments
   B. may make a better adjustment to their assignments if they are in accord with their wishes
   C. may request assignments for which no additional institutional help is required
   D. may not be fitted for the work requested

46. Classification is a dynamic process. According to this statement, it would be MOST reasonable to assume that in the classification process

   A. an inmate's treatment program should be modified in accordance with the changing needs of the inmate
   B. an inmate's treatment program should be carefully planned to avoid the need for changes, or the inmate's cooperation will be lost
   C. interference with, or interruption of, an inmate's treatment program will have serious results
   D. there are very many contributing elements, all equally important, and all of which must operate at maximum efficiency

47. The present trend in penology is to liberalize visiting privileges for inmates as much as possible. However, the MOST important factor that keeps many prison officials from going along with this trend is the fear that liberal prison visiting will

   A. increase the danger of the introduction of contraband into the prison
   B. interfere with the operation of normal prison routines
   C. lead to a breakdown of prison discipline
   D. require major alteration in existing prison facilities for visiting

48. An important rule to be observed in the carrying out of an institutional program of inmate activities and privileges is:
Do not

    A. curtail or revoke any inmate activity or privilege after it has been instituted
    B. give privileges to one inmate which cannot be earned in the proper way by any other inmate
    C. make any activity or privilege too pleasurable for the inmate
    D. use the program as an aid to the maintenance of discipline

48.____

49. Of the following, the MOST important reason for issuing standard prison clothing to all inmates of a sentence institution, rather than permitting them to wear their own civilian clothing, is that it

    A. contributes to the maintenance of better discipline among inmates
    B. eliminates overt, visible differences among inmates which might otherwise lead to friction
    C. is virtually impossible to properly search and sterilize all civilian clothing of all inmates
    D. makes it easier for the public to recognize an escaped inmate

49.____

50. With respect to the operation of a parole system, correctional authorities GENERALLY oppose the

    A. application of strict rules forbidding the parole of persons convicted of certain serious offenses, such as first degree murder and kidnapping
    B. principle that prisoners released from long-term institutions after earning sufficient good time should be released on parole
    C. release of short-term prisoners on parole
    D. requirement of service of a minimum period of imprisonment of reasonable proportions before an inmate becomes eligible for parole

50.____

KEY (CORRECT ANSWERS)

1. D	11. C	21. B	31. D	41. D
2. D	12. A	22. C	32. A	42. C
3. C	13. C	23. D	33. B	43. D
4. A	14. C	24. C	34. A	44. D
5. D	15. A	25. C	35. D	45. B
6. B	16. B	26. A	36. C	46. A
7. C	17. A	27. D	37. D	47. A
8. A	18. B	28. D	38. A	48. B
9. D	19. A	29. B	39. D	49. B
10. C	20. D	30. D	40. B	50. A

TEST 2

DIRECTIONS: Each question or incomplete statement is followed by several suggested answers or completions. Select the one that BEST answers the question or completes the statement. *PRINT THE LETTER OF THE CORRECT ANSWER IN THE SPACE AT THE RIGHT.*

1. It is generally agreed among penologists that the system of communication in an institution should make it possible for any inmate to bring what seems to him an important problem to the attention of an appropriate staff member with the least possible delay. However, a danger to be guarded against in this connection is

   A. artificial separation of lines of authority
   B. a sudden breakdown of administrative control
   C. lack of coordination between professional and custodial staff
   D. misuse of the privilege by unstable inmate personalities

   1.____

2. The one of the following which is NOT an advantage of removing certain classes of inmates from the regular type of prison to outside work on camps and farm colonies is the

   A. ending of direct contact between these inmates and the more undesirable elements in a prison
   B. gradual easing of some of the tensions of prison life for these inmates
   C. removal of the stigma of a prison sentence from these inmates
   D. reduction of inmate idleness in the regular prison

   2.____

3. The suggestion has been advanced that, in correctional systems, the parole board be made a part of the Department of Correction. Of the following, the CHIEF argument in support of this suggestion is that

   A. fullest independence of the parole function and freedom of interference or influence from any source is desirable
   B. lay persons are not sufficiently familiar with correctional problems and procedures to be able to perform this function effectively
   C. since parole is really an extension of the sentence begun in the correctional institution, close integration of the two services is logically desirable
   D. the number of persons placed on parole is not sufficiently large to make administratively feasible the existence of an independent agency

   3.____

4. It has been stated that the quality of the staff in a correctional institution is more important than the physical facilities of the institution. This statement is MOST probably based on the belief that

   A. a basic change in the character of the inmate can be brought about only as a result of the influence and guidance of the staff
   B. a competent staff can achieve excellent results without regard to the physical facilities available
   C. no institution can be run without a staff
   D. the physical facilities of an institution are not important when the staff is highly competent

   4.____

5. In the *cottage* type of correctional institution for women, it is usually considered unnecessary and inappropriate to have disciplinary and custodial controls of the kind customarily found in an institution for men. Of the following, the factor that is LEAST significant in contributing to this difference in this type of women's institution is the

   A. comparative openness of the cottage type institution
   B. difference in preparation and training of the staff
   C. more personal and closer relationship between inmates and staff
   D. small inmate population

6. A feature that makes the *cottage* type institution particularly suitable for female offenders is the

   A. extensive facilities it has for outdoor recreation
   B. opportunities it affords for homemaking activities
   C. practicability of locating near urban centers
   D. privacy offered each individual inmate

7. All correctional institutions for women must accept offenders ranging in age from girls to senile women, and presenting a wide range of sentences and offenses, backgrounds, and training and treatment needs. This is so MAINLY because

   A. female offenders, no less than male offenders, are necessarily different in their characteristics and backgrounds
   B. of the absence and lack of understanding of modern classification procedures
   C. sentencing is a function of the courts, which are neither greatly concerned with nor very much aware of the problems of the correctional administrator
   D. the comparatively small number of women prisoners does not make economically feasible the establishment of diversified institutions for women

8. In the carrying forward of a vocational training program in a women's correctional institution, it will MOST likely be found that those women who have never engaged in systematic training of any kind will

   A. be least eager to participate
   B. be the best learners
   C. have a short interest and concentration span
   D. not make suitable material for such a program

9. Of the following, it is MOST important that the outdoor recreation provided in a correctional institution for women be, as far as possible,

   A. of a competitive, group nature
   B. of the same basic kind and variety as the outdoor recreational activities in an institution for men
   C. of the type that the women can engage in after leaving the institution
   D. limited to non-strenuous activities

10. Of the following, a course that it is particularly important to include in the education program of a correctional institution for women, more so than in a similar program of a correctional institution for men, is a course in

    A. bookkeeping
    B. child guidance
    C. office practice
    D. 3 R's

11. In a correctional institution, inmate discipline is directly associated with morale. Of the following, the CHIEF implication of this statement for the supervisor is that

   A. disciplinary problems are best solved by increasing the inmate's morale
   B. where morale is high, discipline will be maintained more easily
   C. where morale is low, discipline will be found to be lax
   D. where strict disciplinary measures are enforced, morale will be high

12. So small a percentage of all offenders are caught and convicted that what happens to them can have little effect on the great body of potential and actual violators of the law. This statement places GREATEST doubt on the value of _____ as an objective of imprisonment.

   A. deterrence   B. punishment
   C. reformation   D. rehabilitation

13. Suppose that case studies show that rejection by members of an inmate's family has a depressing effect on the inmate's morale. This fact can be used MOST constructively in correctional work to

   A. allow additional privileges to inmates with close family ties
   B. bring family influences to bear in assisting in the inmate's rehabilitation
   C. deny mail and visiting privileges for disciplinary reasons only as a last resort
   D. reveal other media that can be employed to boost the morale of an inmate with no family ties

14. It has been stated that, in the final analysis, the soundest security measure of all is the existence of a positive program of inmate activities. Of the following, the CHIEF justification for this statement is the fact that

   A. a good program of inmate activities will point up the need for correction of certain security weaknesses which might not otherwise be apparent
   B. inmates engaged in such a program of activities seldom resort to disturbances or escape attempts
   C. security without rehabilitation through an inmate program is not a lasting solution to the crime problem
   D. since security is the primary responsibility of the institution, it must be guaranteed by all institutional programs

15. To say that an inmate is psychotic implies MOST directly that the inmate

   A. has a split personality   B. has suicidal tendencies
   C. is mentally deranged   D. is of low mentality

16. A review in the American Journal of Correction of a book about a warden recommended that the book be on the reading list of all students of criminology and penology. The warden about whom this book was written was

   A. Bannan of State Prison of Southern Michigan, Jackson
   B. Ragen of Illinois State Penitentiary, Joliet
   C. Wallack of Wallkill Prison, Wallkill
   D. Wilkinson of U.S. Penitentiary, Atlanta

Questions 17-22.

DIRECTIONS: For each book title in Column I, select the author of the book from Column II; then write the capital letter preceding the author's name in the appropriate space at the right.

	COLUMN I		COLUMN II	
17.	Contemporary Correction	A.	Alexander, Myrl E.	17._____
18.	Criminology, A Cultural Interpretation	B.	Barnes, Harry E.	18._____
19.	Five Hundred Delinquent Women	C.	Fenton, Norman	19._____
20.	Jail Administration	D.	Glueck, Sheldon and Eleanor	20._____
21.	Principles and Methods in Dealing with Offenders	E.	Lindner, Robert M. and Seliger, Robert V.	21._____
22.	Prisoners are People	F.	MacCormick, Austin H.	22._____
		G.	Pigeon, Helen D.	
		H.	Scudder, Kenyon J.	
		J.	Taft, Donald R	
		K.	Tappan, Paul W.	

23. The book WHAT WILL BE YOUR LIFE? is   23._____
    A. a semi-autobiographical sketch written by a former prison inmate
    B. a textbook for prison inmates developed for use in a program of group counseling
    C. directed at potential juvenile delinquents
    D. in use in a pilot program with first offenders on probation

24. A feature of Ident-A-Band, a device for inmate identification, is that it   24._____
    A. cannot be put back if removed
    B. cannot be removed
    C. includes both the fingerprints and photo of the inmate
    D. is worn on the ankle

25. The Congress of Correction is held   25._____
    A. every six months   B. annually
    C. biennially   D. every four years

26. While the court is recessed for lunch, an attorney appears at a Criminal Court detention pen and wishes to pay a fine to secure the release of a defendant. The correction officer at the pen should   26._____

A. accept the fine only if the attorney presents a *Discharge on Payment of Fine* signed by the court clerk and bearing the court seal
B. check the commitment to see that the sentence includes an alternative fine before accepting it
C. refer the attorney to the court clerk
D. send the attorney to the detention prison to which the inmate would be transferred

27. It is a function of the Grand Jury to

   A. determine if a crime has been committed
   B. determine if a defendant is guilty of a crime
   C. secure the evidence necessary to bring an accused to trial
   D. take testimony from the District Attorney and his witnesses as well as from the defendant and his witnesses

28. The MOST accurate of the following statements about the use, form or content of commitments received by the Department of Correction from the Criminal Court is that the

   A. commitment on which a defendant was held for examination will be set aside by another commitment when the defendant is sentenced
   B. form of all commitments is the same
   C. phrase *sentenced that he stand committed to the City Prison, thereafter to be transferred to the workhouse for a period of* appears on a short commitment
   D. phrase *is committed to your custody pending examination or trial on* appears on a full commitment

29. The purpose of the *court recall sheet* is to

   A. list the inmates against whom there are other holds upon expiration of their present sentences
   B. list the inmates to be transferred from the court pen to the detention prison
   C. notify the court clerk of inmates who must be returned to prison even if released by the court on charge being heard
   D. notify the warden that he must produce certain named inmates in court or before the Grand Jury on a given date

30. When a judge exercises summary jurisdiction in a police case, he may

   A. commit the defendant to the Department of Correction pending further examination
   B. find the defendant guilty and impose sentence
   C. hold the defendant for a higher court
   D. hold the defendant for the Grand Jury

31. The MOST accurate of the following statements about the jurisdiction or functioning of the Criminal Court is that they

   A. cannot convict and sentence defendants arraigned but can merely hold them for other courts
   B. cannot sit as Courts of Special Sessions
   C. conduct preliminary examinations to determine whether defendants should be held for the Grand Jury or the Supreme Court
   D. rank second of the lower courts in volume of cases handled

32. The form which serves as the alphabetical register of all inmates in a Department institution is the _____ Card.

    A. Accompanying
    B. Inmate's Record
    C. Institution Locator
    D. Prisoner's Registration

33. A correction officer in a Criminal Court detention pen may permit an attorney to visit a defendant who is his client if the

    A. attorney presents a *Notice of Appearance* signed by the court clerk
    B. attorney presents a *Notice to the Warden* from the committing court
    C. defendant gives written consent
    D. visit has been cleared with and authorized by the warden of the appropriate detention prison

34. When an inmate is committed to the Department by the court on two charges, it is important that the notation *two cases* be written on records relating to the inmate MAINLY to

    A. avoid errors in daily census
    B. insure that the inmate is counted as one admission in the compilation of Department statistics
    C. insure that two commitments have been issued
    D. prevent release of the inmate before both charges have been disposed of

35. Of the following, the CHIEF reason for encouraging inmates to read, study, engage in some worthwhile hobby, or learn a trade while in prison is to help

    A. prevent major disturbances among inmates
    B. inmates forget about their punishment
    C. inmates adjust to normal life when released
    D. increase inmates' interests
    E. pass away the long hours of confinement

36. Of the following, the MOST accurate statement concerning short-term sentences is that they

    A. usually provide an opportunity to rehabilitate the minor criminal
    B. are relatively ineffective in giving the prisoner a new outlook on life
    C. are the answer to many baffling problems presented to a penal institution
    D. have been on the decrease in the United States since 1900
    E. offer adequate opportunity for moral, but not vocational, rehabilitation

37. If inmates are transferred from one institution of the Department to another, the receiving institution can quickly know the court history of these inmates during the time of their custody at any institution of the Department from their

    A. accompanying cards
    B. commitments
    C. locator cards
    D. registration cards

38. Of the following, the factor that is LEAST significant in making the problem of custody and control in a trial prison more difficult than in a sentence prison is the

    A. comparative absence of program for inmates in a trial prison
    B. different educational and social background of inmates in a trial prison

C. different legal status of trial inmates
D. heterogeneity of inmates in a trial prison

39. Of the trial inmates confined in the detention prisons, a comparison of inmates charged with misdemeanors with inmates charged with felonies shows that GENERALLY those charged with

   A. felonies are confined for shorter periods of time while awaiting trial
   B. misdemeanors are easier to control as a group
   C. felonies are in poorer physical condition
   D. misdemeanors have a lower rate of recidivism

40. With respect to communication between trial inmates and their relatives or friends on the outside, the supervisor should advise correction officers that

   A. they must closely supervise all telephone calls made by trial inmates
   B. they must make all the entries on the telephone message form carefully as it is a permanent record
   C. inmates who do not have the money to pay for a call must be given stationery to communicate by mail
   D. the right of such communication is guaranteed to trial inmates by law

41. According to the provisions of the Criminal Courts Act, persons committed to the reformatory

   A. are released at the discretion of the Parole Commission
   B. are sentenced for terms of 1 to 3 years
   C. may be felons or misdemeanants
   D. must be between the ages of 16 and 25

42. According to an analysis of attempted suicides in the institutions of the Department,

   A. most attempted suicides occur on the midnight to 8 A.M. tour of duty
   B. most attempted suicides occur on the 8 A.M. to 4 P.M. tour of duty
   C. most attempted suicides occur on the 4 P.M. to midnight tour of duty
   D. there are approximately the same number of attempted suicides on each of the three tours of duty

43. According to Department statistics, the greatest number of escapes and attempted escapes occurs on the 8 A.M. to 4 P.M. tour. This is MOST probably due to the fact that

   A. conditions are most conducive to escape when there is the greatest amount of institutional activity
   B. often escapes actually committed at night are not discovered until the next day, resulting in inaccurate statistics
   C. on a comparative basis, more personnel should be assigned to the day tour to enforce adequate security
   D. there is a relaxation of custodial supervision on the day tour, resulting in lowered security

44. Of the following, the CHIEF reason why the Department of Correction no longer considered a certain reformatory suitable for its purposes was probably that   44.____

    A. its physical plant was too big for the relatively small and select inmate population
    B. its physical plant was too old, dating back to the previous century
    C. it was proving insufficiently secure for the changing type of adolescent inmate the Department was getting
    D. it had no facilities for a satisfactory vocational program in urban occupations

45. The Department's adolescent program for youths in detention is concentrated on the age group   45.____

    A. 18 to 30   B. 16 to 30   C. 16 to 25   D. 16 to 20

46. The CHIEF value of team games, as opposed to individual sports, as a form of recreation in prisons is that they   46.____

    A. are easier to teach
    B. emphasize the social element
    C. are more enjoyable
    D. permit spectator participation
    E. cause the individual to develop skill more rapidly

47. It is generally held that, with reference to type of treatment afforded prisoners, the average American county jail is   47.____

    A. the most neglected of our penal and correctional institutions
    B. on a par with the state prison
    C. better than the state prison
    D. as good as the Federal prison
    E. remarkably in advance of general practice in penology

48. The type of control through which the behavior of an inmate is BEST directed is _____ control.   48.____

    A. group   B. imposed   C. leader
    D. self   E. dictatorial

49. John Smith has been a dope fiend for 12 years. He has served three jail sentences and paid several fines for selling dope. Today is his last day of a six-month jail sentence for having dope in his possession.
    He will MOST probably   49.____

    A. realize that his addiction to dope only brings him shame and disgrace and never use dope again
    B. begin using dope again in a short time
    C. have a high regard for law and order in the future
    D. have greater regard for the rights of other members of the community
    E. become a respectable citizen if he moves to a community where he is relatively unknown

50. Of the following, the BEST procedure to follow when an inmate has a temper tantrum while with a group of other inmates is, in general, to

 A. separate him from the group
 B. warn him that you will have to send for the warden
 C. appeal to his pride before the others
 D. reprimand him loudly
 E. advise him that he may be punished with solitary confinement

KEY (CORRECT ANSWERS)

1. D	11. B	21. G	31. C	41. A
2. C	12. A	22. H	32. C	42. C
3. C	13. B	23. B	33. B	43. A
4. A	14. B	24. A	34. D	44. D
5. B	15. C	25. B	35. C	45. D
6. B	16. B	26. C	36. B	46. B
7. D	17. K	27. A	37. A	47. A
8. C	18. J	28. A	38. B	48. D
9. C	19. D	29. D	39. B	49. B
10. B	20. A	30. B	40. D	50. A

TEST 3

DIRECTIONS: Each question or incomplete statement is followed by several suggested answers or completions. Select the one that BEST answers the question or completes the statement. *PRINT THE LETTER OF THE CORRECT ANSWER IN THE SPACE AT THE RIGHT.*

1. Suppose that a correction officer disagrees with the procedure which you, as supervisor, have outlined for him to follow in carrying out a certain assignment. Of the following, it is MOST desirable for you to tell this officer that

    A. in a semi-military organization orders must be carried out or discipline will be impaired
    B. the procedure you have outlined has been used successfully for many years in the past
    C. you are merely carrying out the orders of your own superior
    D. you will evaluate his objections to the procedure you have outlined

    1.____

2. An officer under your supervision refers to you for solution routine problems that arise on his post which other officers usually take care of themselves. Of the following, it would be MOST desirable for you to

    A. ask a more experienced employee to assist this officer whenever he has a problem
    B. show this officer when he refers a routine matter how to handle it himself and encourage him to do so in the future
    C. tell this officer to stand on his own two feet and assume his fair share of responsibility
    D. temporarily assign this officer to another post with less responsibility until he develops the capacity to handle his job properly

    2.____

3. A correction officer under your supervision regularly submits considerably more infraction reports against inmates than other officers with similar posts. Of the following, the MOST desirable action for you to take would be to

    A. direct this officer to be fairer toward the inmates
    B. give this officer additional training in order to strengthen his disciplinary control over the inmates
    C. reprimand this officer for his poor control over the inmates
    D. take no special action since in any such ranking there must always be one officer at the top and one at the bottom

    3.____

4. A correction superior gave his officers special training in the detection and prevention of suicides among prison inmates. Nevertheless, there still occurred two inmate suicides in his command during the year. Therefore, it would be MOST desirable for the superior to

    A. analyze the two suicides in order to develop special methods for preventing similar occurrences in the future
    B. assign a double guard to all suspected suicides
    C. change his training methods as they were obviously defective
    D. realize that there is a certain irreducible minimum of such occurrences which cannot be eliminated

    4.____

5. An efficient supervisor will make it a routine part of his job to study the inmates, whether he is assigned to a court pen, detention prison, penitentiary, reformatory or hospital ward. Of the following, the MOST direct implication of the preceding statement is that

    A. a good supervisor knows the habits of the inmates he supervises
    B. an efficient supervisor can successfully perform any assignment
    C. diversification of institutions for inmates is becoming more common
    D. the study of inmates, though not difficult, is often neglected

6. A new officer asks you for advice as to what to do if an inmate should refuse to carry out an order. As supervisor, you should advise this officer to

    A. ask himself if the order was a reasonable one
    B. avoid being drawn into a situation of this kind
    C. immediately summon his superior for assistance
    D. warn the prisoner that he will be subject to disciplinary action

7. A superior advised correction officers to prepare a schedule for the daily patrol of their posts and to adhere to this schedule every day. The superior's advice was

    A. *bad,* because the element of surprise is an important aid to successful detection of forbidden activities
    B. *bad,* because the inmates should always be kept guessing as to the officer's next move
    C. *good,* because regular habits, a desirable trait in a correction officer, will be developed
    D. *good,* because the inmate should be made to realize that he is always under observation

8. A superior assigned to a mess hall where several hundred inmates are eating their supper meal observes an inmate commit an infraction of the rules which does not immediately jeopardize the welfare of any officer or inmate.
Of the following, it would be BEST for the superior to

    A. defer disciplinary action until the inmates are returned to their cells in order to avoid the danger of precipitating a disturbance
    B. overlook the incident if nothing more serious happens as it may be part of a deliberate plan to stage a demonstration
    C. reprimand the offender at once to show the other inmates that he is in control of the situation
    D. warn the inmate that he will be subject to disciplinary action later because punishment, to be effective, must be prompt

9. A supervisor advised a new correction officer not to permit inmates to address him by his first name. The supervisor's advice was

    A. *bad,* because it creates a wider gap than necessary between officer and inmate
    B. *bad,* because no rule is applicable in every situation
    C. *good,* because familiarity between officer and inmate may lead to a breakdown of discipline
    D. *good,* because the more impersonally an inmate is treated the easier he is to control

10. An officer under your supervision reports to you that he suspects a certain inmate of suicidal tendencies. Of the following, the BEST action for you to take FIRST in this situation is to

    A. have the officer prepare a report for forwarding to your superior
    B. re-arrange the inmate's program so that he is always in the company of another inmate
    C. talk to the inmate and keep him under observation for a while in order to verify the accuracy of the officer's suspicions
    D. transfer the inmate to another cell where he may be kept under constant observation

11. A supervisor observes a correction officer deny an inmate's request to go to the medical clinic. This inmate has made similar requests in the past without cause and appears to have nothing the matter with him now. The supervisor should evaluate the officer's action as

    A. *unsound,* because if the inmate is really sick the denial of the request may have serious results
    B. *unsound,* because an officer should never be influenced by an inmate's previous record
    C. *sound,* because if the inmate is really sick he will let the officer know it soon enough
    D. *sound,* because it takes into account the inmate's previous record

12. On a tour of posts you observe that in a cell block supervised by a new officer, the line-up of inmates before reporting for work assignments is proceeding in a slow and disorderly manner. In this situation, it is MOST desirable that you, as supervisor,

    A. call the officer's attention to the fact that the line-up is not proceeding properly and then continue with your tour of posts
    B. issue a mild reprimand and take personal command of the line-up in order to prevent further confusion
    C. make a mental note of the situation and discuss the proper way of conducting a line-up at the next conference with your officers
    D. take the officer aside and instruct him in the immediate action to take in order to correct this situation

13. Of the following, it is MOST desirable that a supervisor train correction officers to

    A. carry out all assignments in a thorough-going and business-like manner
    B. impress upon inmates as soon as they are admitted that breaches of discipline will not be tolerated
    C. interpret inmates' behavior in terms of impressions formed upon admission
    D. learn all the rules and regulations thoroughly so as to be able to answer quickly any question raised by an inmate

14. Two of the officers under your supervision, who are assigned to a common post, are in frequent conflict with each other. In this situation, it is MOST desirable that you

    A. direct the officers to stop their arguments as they are interfering with efficient performance
    B. discuss with the officers the basic reasons for their conflict

C. tell both officers to refer all disputes to you for settlement
D. transfer one of the officers to another post

15. Of the following, the MOST desirable procedure for a supervisor to follow in order to keep correction officers *on their toes* is to

    A. apply disciplinary measures for the violation of department rules and regulations impartially
    B. encourage initiative by delegating responsibility to the best officers
    C. require them to prepare and submit frequent reports on their activities
    D. test their knowledge and alertness frequently

16. Suppose that on organized tier searches for contraband more contraband is usually found on the post of one officer under your command than on the post of any other officer. The one of the following which is MOST likely to be an important contributing factor in this situation is the

    A. amount of time this officer has devoted to the study of his book of rules
    B. amount of training you have given your staff in the detection and control of contraband smuggling
    C. special problems inherent in the type of post commanded by this officer
    D. thoroughness with which the different types of posts are searched

17. The one of the following which would probably contribute MOST to obtaining the maximum cooperation of subordinates in carrying out a change in a long established procedure would be to

    A. give several weeks advance notice of the proposed change in procedure
    B. hold staff conferences to explain and discuss the changed procedure prior to its adoption
    C. make provision for abandoning the new procedure if it is not accepted by the majority of the staff
    D. refrain from enforcing absolute compliance with the new procedure at the very beginning

18. Suppose that mail received by inmates of an institution of the Department is censored in a mail censoring room and then forwarded to the cell tier officer for distribution to the inmates. As supervisor, you should instruct the tier officer to

    A. distribute this mail to the inmates immediately upon receipt as it has already been censored carefully
    B. notify you whenever any mail is received by a former drug addict
    C. quickly examine the contents of each letter again as a double check before giving it to the inmate
    D. remove any enclosures which may not have been removed by the mail censor

19. A supervisor advised correction officers to approach with caution any inmate whose behavior was in any way different from normal. The supervisor's advice was

    A. *bad*, because over-caution on the part of a correction officer may be taken by the inmates as a sign of fear
    B. *bad*, because the inmate may actually be in need of immediate attention

C. *good,* because even seemingly harmless abnormal behavior may be part of a prepared plan for an attack
D. *good,* because every action of an inmate should be looked upon with mistrust

20. A supervisor detailed to assigning inmates to institutional work details should, in arriving at a decision as to the best assignment for an inmate, give LEAST consideration to the inmate's

    A. economic status
    B. educational background
    C. medical history
    D. occupational history

21. A new correction officer asks you to explain why department regulations permit officers to carry firearms only when having custody of a prisoner outside the prison, and not while on duty within the prison. Of the following, the BEST explanation of the justification for this rule is that

    A. an inmate has greater opportunities for escape when outside the prison walls
    B. an officer is not likely to be attacked by an inmate within the institution
    C. a single officer usually has custody of a prisoner outside the prison, whereas inside the prison there are always other officers present to render assistance in case of trouble
    D. firearms are dangerous weapons in the hands of inexperienced or unstable officers

22. A supervisor advised a correction officer as follows: When you take a count of inmates locked in a tier of cells, keep your eyes at such an angle as to have the occupant of the next cell in your line of vision immediately after verifying the count of the preceding cell. The advice of the supervisor was

    A. *bad,* because it is physically impossible to keep the eyes at the angle recommended
    B. *bad,* because when taking a count undivided attention to the cell being checked is essential
    C. *good,* because a surprise attack by the inmate in the next cell can better be prevented
    D. *good,* because in this way the process of taking the count will be speeded up

23. A supervisor directed correction officers to forbid inmates to accumulate back issues of magazines and newspapers in their cells. The supervisor's order was

    A. *bad,* because each inmate's case should be treated individually
    B. *bad,* because it discriminates against the inmate who likes to devote leisure time to reading
    C. *good,* because an accumulation of such material in cells is a health and fire hazard
    D. *good,* because an inmate does not have enough leisure time to read so much material anyway

24. Of the following, it is MOST desirable that a supervisor train correction officers to

    A. have no fear
    B. never depend on others for assistance
    C. obey all orders without question
    D. think before they act

25. As supervisor, you are assigned a detail of officers with whom to conduct a search of a tier of cells for contraband.
Of the following, the MOST desirable action for you to take in carrying out this assignment is to

   A. brief the officers of the detail in any special procedure to be followed in this case
   B. confer with the tier officer the day before as to which cells should receive closest attention
   C. have the entire detail of officers enter one cell at a time and search it thoroughly before proceeding to the next one
   D. notify the officer and inmates of the tier in advance of the search that they will have to be moved temporarily so that the search can be carried out with the least interference

26. A correction officer on a tour of inspection at night failed to observe any signs of life in the occupant of one cell. The officer immediately entered the cell to check further. When the officer reported this action to the supervisor, the latter was very critical. The supervisor's criticism was

   A. *justified,* because it wasn't necessary to enter the cell in order to find out if the inmate was dead
   B. *justified,* because the officer should not have entered the cell alone
   C. *unjustified,* because the officer had shown alertness and should have been praised
   D. *unjustified,* because the officer may have been unable to get help quickly at night

27. Suppose that a supervisor is required to review disciplinary reports against inmates prepared by correction officers before forwarding them to the disciplinary officer. Of the following, the report which it is MOST desirable for the supervisor to return to the correction officer for rewriting is one which

   A. fails to employ a high standard of written English
   B. fails to recommend an appropriate punishment
   C. is incomplete as to main details
   D. relates to more than one inmate

28. In a correctional institution where inmates were issued a manual of the rules, regulations, and procedures of the prison, a superior supplemented the manual by having the inmates given oral instruction in these matters upon admission. Of the following, the LEAST important reason for giving such supplemental oral instruction is that

   A. inmates can thereby be informed of new rules or changes in old rules
   B. inmates may not take the trouble to read the manual
   C. prison inmates occasionally lack the mentality to grasp even the most simply written instructions
   D. some prison inmates cannot read well enough

29. Newly appointed correction personnel should be given training of the orientation type, as well as training in their duties and in the application to their new positions of techniques or skills already acquired. Of the following topics, the one which BEST illustrates the first type of training described above is:

   A. Fundamentals of Supervisory Technique
   B. Purposes of Correctional Treatment

C. Required Dress for Correction Officers
D. The Daily Institutional Schedule

30. There are many methods of maintaining discipline among prison inmates. However, that discipline is best which disciplines least. Of the following, the MOST valid inference based on the preceding statement is that a correction supervisor should

A. apply punitive measures only when unavoidable
B. apply the least severe punitive measure when more than one is applicable
C. have discipline rest mainly on good morale rather than on strict enforcement of detailed rules and regulations
D. leave the disciplining of inmates to the correction officers and interfere only when called upon by them for assistance or advice

31. Only the highest type of officer should be assigned to the receiving room of a detention prison. Of the following, the BEST justification for this statement is that

A. in this assignment an officer is exposed to many pressures
B. the inmate's future conduct in prison may be decided by the first impression formed upon admission
C. the routine of administration in the receiving room of a detention prison is more complex
D. this may be the only contact with prison life for most prisoners

32. We should beware of assuming that a new jail necessarily means a good penal institution. This statement implies MOST directly that

A. not all good penal institutions are new
B. not all old jails are bad penal institutions
C. some new jails are not good penal institutions
D. some old jails are good penal institutions

33. A good probation department, by furnishing the judge with information regarding the guilty individual, makes possible discrimination in the use of imprisonment and, in the person of the probation officer, provides a substitute for it. Of the following, the MOST direct implication of the preceding statement is that

A. a properly functioning probation department offers the means for effective use of probation in lieu of imprisonment for some offenders
B. if used with discrimination by the judge, probation is sometimes in itself an indirect form of punishment
C. probation, as a substitute for imprisonment, should be more widely used
D. the primary function of a good probation officer is to secure background information about the offender

34. The fact that the offense is not serious does not mean that the perpetrator can be easily turned into a law-abiding citizen. Of the following, the BEST evidence in support of this statement is the

A. high rate of recidivism among misdemeanant prisoners
B. large number of small jails
C. number of prisoners who violate parole
D. reluctance of society to accept the former convict

35. The chain of prison administration is only as strong as its weakest officer. The preceding statement implies MOST directly that

   A. careful selection and proper training of personnel are not sufficiently emphasized by many prison administrators
   B. every prison employee is basically an administrator
   C. one inefficient officer can sometimes seriously impair the functioning of an entire institution
   D. the chainlike organization of prison management becomes apparent when a weak officer fails to perform his job properly

36. The industrial farm is the best type of institution yet developed for the majority of jail prisoners. Of the following, the BEST justification for this statement is that in an institution of this type

   A. strictest application of advanced classification procedures is possible
   B. the products of inmate labor in large measure pay for the cost of running the institution
   C. there is likely to be freedom from political interference because it is located away from urban centers
   D. worthwhile employment and training in desirable surroundings can be afforded every inmate

37. Several studies have shown that the majority of sentenced workhouse prisoners are recidivists. Of the following, the MOST valid inference based on the preceding statement is that

   A. commitment procedures for certain classes of prisoners should be re-studied
   B. for many prisoners custody, rather than rehabilitation, should be emphasized
   C. the rate of recidivism is greatest among workhouse prisoners
   D. while prison administrators give more attention to rehabilitative measures today, results are generally poor

38. It is desirable that the prisoners be well acquainted with the practices and procedures of the parole board. Of the following, the BEST argument in favor of this policy is that

   A. parole practices and procedures often change with a change in the make-up of the parole board
   B. prisoner participation in the formulation of parole board practices and procedures is desirable
   C. prisoners will be less prone to think they were unjustly treated by the parole board
   D. the parole board will be less subject to public criticism

39. Of the following, the MOST probable reason why public criticism of recreational programs for prisoners is much less common today than it was twenty-five years ago is that the general public nowadays

   A. accepts the rehabilitative objectives of correctional institutions more readily
   B. comprehends the real value of recreation in the correctional program
   C. is more interested in recreation and sports
   D. understands the problems involved in the maintenance of prison discipline

40. Of the following, the CHIEF value of the indeterminate sentence is that 40.____

    A. better discipline is obtained from the prisoner during the period of his incarceration
    B. the length of time to be served can be adjusted to the seriousness of the crime
    C. the sentencing power of the courts is curtailed
    D. the time spent in jail can be related to the rate of rehabilitative progress

41. Suppose that a study of prison inmates shows that a relatively small percentage of first 41.____
    offenders become second offenders, but that a very large percentage of second offenders commit subsequent offenses. Of the following, the LEAST valid inference based on the study described is that

    A. correctional procedures presently employed with second offenders are largely ineffective
    B. first offenders offer the most fertile field for rehabilitative efforts
    C. in a random sampling of prisoners, most of those sampled will have committed two or more offenses
    D. it is more difficult to attain success in the rehabilitation of second offenders than in the rehabilitation of first offenders

42. The mess hall is usually considered by prison administrators as the most sensitive spot 42.____
    in a correctional institution MAINLY because

    A. a large number of inmates is gathered together there at one time
    B. an insufficient number of officers is often assigned to the mess hall during meal periods
    C. the food in most prisons is inadequate and poorly prepared
    D. the use of eating utensils as weapons can be dangerous

43. Progressive penologists GENERALLY are of the opinion that 43.____

    A. alcoholics should be sentenced to jail for at least six months so that a cure can be effected
    B. alcoholics should receive an indeterminate rather than a definite jail term
    C. chronic alcoholism is a sickness rather than a crime
    D. treatment for chronic alcoholism should be made compulsory

44. It has been proposed that wider use be made of fines in lieu of imprisonment as a 44.____
    method of punishment for certain offenses. Of the following, the BEST argument in support of this proposal is that

    A. contact with prison atmosphere is often an effective deterrent to a repetition of the offense
    B. fines are not difficult to collect
    C. fines can be adjusted to the ability of the offender to pay
    D. imprisonment is expensive for the government

45. Penologists are generally opposed to the use of force as a method of maintaining prison 45.____
    discipline MAINLY because

    A. it is difficult to limit its use to self-defense or the enforcement of lawful commands
    B. it is of doubtful legality

C. modern escape-proof institutions have reduced the discipline problem to a minimum
D. resentment of the use of force by inmates may create, rather than correct, discipline problems

46. Of the following, the MAIN reason why it is so difficult to eradicate the smuggling of narcotics into a prison is that

    A. it is not possible to measure the personal integrity of prison personnel prior to their appointment to the service
    B. so many prison inmates are drug addicts today
    C. there are so many possible ways for the drugs to enter the prison
    D. the supply of available drugs is constantly increasing

47. Of the following, the LEAST valid argument in favor of having a commissary in a correctional institution is that the commissary

    A. contributes to the maintenance of inmate morale
    B. helps to reduce the institution's food budget
    C. is an important aid in maintaining discipline
    D. provides funds, not otherwise available, to buy recreational equipment for inmates

48. Of the following, the CHIEF argument in favor of dormitories over cells as a method of housing prison inmates is that dormitories

    A. are cheaper to construct
    B. are easier to clean
    C. make custodial supervision easier
    D. are preferred by inmates

49. In comparing the Pennsylvania with the Auburn system of penal discipline, it is MOST correct to state that in the

    A. Auburn system the prisoners were completely separated from each other except at meal time
    B. Auburn system the prisoners were not permitted to talk to each other
    C. Pennsylvania system prison visiting was prohibited
    D. Pennsylvania system the prisoners were allowed to mingle with each other only when at work

50. The proper Fahrenheit temperature which should be maintained in a cell block during the winter months is MOST NEARLY

    A. 60°   B. 65°   C. 73°   D. 75°

KEY (CORRECT ANSWERS)

1. D	11. A	21. A	31. B	41. C
2. B	12. D	22. C	32. C	42. A
3. B	13. A	23. C	33. A	43. C
4. A	14. B	24. D	34. A	44. D
5. A	15. D	25. A	35. C	45. D
6. D	16. C	26. B	36. D	46. C
7. A	17. B	27. C	37. A	47. B
8. A	18. C	28. A	38. C	48. A
9. C	19. C	29. B	39. A	49. B
10. C	20. A	30. C	40. D	50. B

EXAMINATION SECTION
TEST 1

DIRECTIONS: Each question or incomplete statement is followed by several suggested answers or completions. Select the one that BEST answers the question or completes the statement. *PRINT THE LETTER OF THE CORRECT ANSWER IN THE SPACE AT THE RIGHT.*

1. The way the custodial prison maintains stability of life within its walls is

    A. through the granting of privileges
    B. through the exercise of total power by guards
    C. by treating all inmates alike, in order to destroy the influence of inmate leaders
    D. by dealing with leaders chosen by the inmates

1.____

2. A prison has been described as a *total institution* in which large groups of persons live together around the clock within a circumscribed space under a tightly scheduled sequence of activities imposed by a central authority. Of the following, the MOST likely consequence of this way of life is that

    A. effective rehabilitation is easily achieved
    B. deviant behavior is unlikely to occur
    C. correctional staff and inmates will develop hostile sterotypes of each other
    D. change in the social relationships in prisons can occur if all signs of a punitive ideology are removed

2.____

3. Daily interaction between inmates and guards results in

    A. coercion of inmates by guards
    B. a tendency toward corruption of authority
    C. a desire of guards to act as policemen, and not as work foremen
    D. an increase in aloof behavior between inmates and guards

3.____

4. Studies on the Jukes and Kallikaks reflected a certain intellectual atmosphere. The one of the following statements which BEST states this atmosphere is that

    A. crime is interrelated with the social and cultural systems of total society
    B. criminal behavior is a product of the lack of religious upbringing
    C. The individual is fundamentally influenced by his family and friends
    D. criminal behavior is inherited

4.____

5. The indeterminate sentence sets

    A. a fixed maximum term and usually a fixed minimum
    B. a fixed maximum term but no minimum
    C. a fixed minimum term but no maximum
    D. neither minimum nor maximum terms

5.____

6. The *good time* system of permitting a reduction in the prisoner's sentence of an established number of days for each year of good behavior has been

6.____

A. applied in a manner which carefully discriminates between prison-wise and rehabilitation-oriented prisoners
B. accepted by most prisoners as a method of rewarding their good behavior and punishing their misbehavior
C. applied to prisoners who are assigned to routine jobs but not to those who perform such crucial jobs as cooking or maintenance
D. undermined as a rehabilitative tool by the mechanical way in which its awards are granted

7. The percent of all personnel working in local jails and institutions nationally who devote their time to treatment and training is, MOST NEARLY,

   A. 3%   B. 15%   C. 30%   D. 60%

8. To the greatest possible extent, correctional rehabilitation should be a *joint* responsibility of

   A. government and private agencies
   B. police and correction staff
   C. custodial and professional staff
   D. staff and inmates

9. Persons who are released from prison are LEAST likely to commit new crimes if they were originally convicted of which of the following?

   A. Auto theft
   B. Robbery
   C. Narcotics offenses
   D. Serious crimes of violence

10. Inmates who are referred to as *right guys* or *straights* are

    A. inmates reutinely thrown into very personal contact with staff
    B. at the lowest stratum of the inmate society
    C. likely to be suspected by other inmates if they have private communication with staff
    D. the inmates who most personify the *aggressive convict*

11. Many states are reporting new trends in inmate counseling. The one of the following which indicates *one* of these new trends is the

    A. use of professionals to direct and supervise sub-professionals who are performing the direct treatment task
    B. elimination of individual counseling and substitution of orientation interviews in its place
    C. movement of specialists out of dormitories and cell blocks and into special counseling rooms
    D. use of traditional psychotherapeutic efforts as the only counseling procedure

12. In recent years, corrections has seen the development of new operating methods designed to create a more *collaborative* institution which is less isolated from the community physically and in terms of values. Which of the following is LEAST likely to be part of this trend toward *collaborative* institutions?

    A. Group counseling involving institutional employees and groups of inmates
    B. Inmate involvement in institution management groups

C. Use of selected inmates to help guard and control other inmates
D. Institutional construction that emphasizes small rooms housing one inmate each

13. Changing corrections into a system with significantly increased power to reduce recidivism and prevent recruitment into criminal careers will require, above all else, many tasks to be done.
    Of the following, the MOST reasonable inference which can be drawn from this statement is that

    A. most personnel in corrections are custody-oriented
    B. the main ingredient for changing people is other people
    C. training of correctional personnel has been uniformly inadequate
    D. the barriers imposed by the criminal label make rehabilitation difficult to achieve

14. The MOST promising correctional strategy today is

    A. probation   B. institutionalization
    C. parole   D. halfway programs

15. One of the MOST critical problems in developing new community-based programs has been the

    A. antagonism of staff to such programs
    B. lack of acceptance of such programs by the community
    C. conflict between staff and inmates over methods of implementing such programs
    D. negative attitude of inmates toward such programs

Questions 16 - 25.

DIRECTIONS: Each of Question 16 through 25 consists of two statements. Choose answer
    A. if both statements are correct
    B. if neither statement is correct
    C. if statement I only is correct but not statement II
    D. if statement II only is correct but not statement I

16. I. A complaint is an allegation of an improper or unlawful act of omission which relates to the business of the department.
    II. A member of the department who is not a superior officer may not make a complaint of dereliction of duty against another member of the department.

17. I. Changes or additions to the rules and regulations shall be promulgated by a special order of the department, and any change or addition shall be stated in full therein.
    II. Employees of the central office of the department shall, in the performance of their duties, be subject to the direction and control of the heads of the divisions to which they are assigned

18. I. Whenever an inmate, upon first admission to an institution, or return from outside the institution, refuses to be fingerprinted, photographed or submit to a clothing and body search for contraband, reasonable force shall be used immediately to compel him to do so.
    II. Except as required by his official duties, a member of the department shall not correspond with prisoners or former prisoners.

19. I. When an inmate is taken for treatment to any clinic which is accessible to the general public, he shall be handcuffed during the course of treatment, except when a physician or other competent person administering treatment requests that the handcuffs be removed.
    II. All matters concerning the welfare of an employee, which requires the attention of the central office, must be submitted in writing through the head of the institution.

19.___

20. I. Except when required as a part of their prescribed duties, employees assigned to the various institutions of the department will not telephone or visit central office without the express permission or direction of the respective heads of institutions.
    II. No superseding commitment will be accepted by a member of the department in the case of an inmate committed to serve a sentence in an institution of the department.

20.___

21. I. Line-ups for the purpose of identification of any inmate or inmates shall be conducted whenever requested in writing by the Police Department.
    II. Whenever a member of the department is directed by the medical director to consult his personal physician for the treatment of a condition which impairs his efficiency as a member of the department, he shall take prompt action to obtain such treatment. Failure to do so shall be deemed neglect of duty.

21.___

22. I. A member of the department shall have recorded with the head of the institution or division his correct residence, phone number, and social status, and shall promptly report any change in the foregoing.
    II. It shall be the duty of a member of the department charged with the custody of inmates at any time or place, to make an oral report of any conduct against good order and descipline by an iamate.

22.___

23. I. Members of the department shall not be granted permission to peruse their personal history folder when matters of a derogatory nature are to be filed therein.
    II. Whenever an order is received from the court for the discharge of an inmate, or his sentence expires, while said inmate is being held in a court detention pen, he shall be transferred to an institution for discharge.

23.___

24. I. No member of the department shall engage in any business or transaction or shall have a financial or other private interest, direct or indirect, which is in conflict with the proper discharge of his official duties.
    II. Under special circumstances, a correction officer may make cell, tier, floor or dormitory assignments of inmates, or change such assignments.

24.___

25. I. When it is deemed necessary at any time to search the person of any employee on duty, such search shall be made by a captain or other superior officer.
    II. Mechanical means of physical restraint other than handcuffs shall be used only when necessary in transporting prisoners, or under medical advice when necessary to prevent injury to the prisoner or to others.

25.___

KEY (CORRECT ANSWERS)

1.	A	11.	A
2.	C	12.	C
3.	B	13.	B
4.	D	14.	A
5.	D	15.	B
6.	D	16.	C
7.	A	17.	D
8.	D	18.	D
9.	D	19.	A
10.	C	20.	A

21. D
22. C
23. B
24. C
25. A

TEST 2

DIRECTIONS: Each question or incomplete statement is followed by several suggested answers or completions. Select the one that BEST answers the question or completes the statement. *PRINT THE LETTER OF THE CORRECT ANSWER IN THE SPACE AT THE RIGHT.*

1. The degree of security needed for the confinement of an inmate depends upon the   1.___

    A. calibre of personnel assigned to the institution
    B. personality and background of the inmate
    C. type of programs available in the institution
    D. type of security facilities within the institution

2. The one of the following which is an example of partial institutional custody is   2.___

    A. civil commitment
    B. conditional release
    C. probation
    D. work release

3. With regard to the custodial aspect of the criminal treatment system, which of the following is recommended?   3.___

    A. Administration of probation by the judiciary, and administration of incarceration and parole by the executive branch
    B. Greater emphasis on the difference between incarceration and the field services (probation and parole)
    C. Placing few offenders in the community as soon as possible in order to reduce the risk that they will commit new crimes
    D. Development of a single overall concept of custody which eliminates the arbitrary lines between probation, incarceration and parole

4. In the context of the criminal treatment system, the term *sanction* comprises formal community condemnation, deprivation of rights and privileges, and forfeiture of property for a purpose other than restitution or reparation, imposed and carried out by the state as a direct consequence of conduct that violates a prohibition promulgated by the state. Which of the following is NOT a sanction in the context of the criminal treatment system?   4.___

    A. Conditional discharge
    B. Conviction
    C. Incarceration
    D. Field supervision

5. According to *Attica: The Official Report of the New York State Special Commission on Attica,* when negotiations between inmates and officials failed in the 1971 uprising in Attica,   5.___

    A. inmates advised state officials that they expected guns to be used to retake the institution but that such a move would prove futile since inmates had full access to the Attica armory
    B. state officials assured inmates that no force would be used in retaking the institution until after the Governor had met with the inmate committee
    C. state officials did not advise inmates that they intended to retake the institution with guns nor did they make adequate arrangements for the medical care of severe casualties
    D. state officials were told by the Governor that, if any of the hostages were injured or killed, guns should be used in storming the prison

6. In the Attica report, the Commission states that one out of every _____ residents of New York City was a victim of crime in 1971.
Which one of the following, when inserted in the blank space, makes the statement CORRECT?

    A. four
    B. fifteen
    C. thirty-seven
    D. seventy-five

7. According to a recent issue of the American Journal of Correction, medical experimentation in correctional institutions has become a major focus of attention. The article shows how the Connecticut Department of Corrections has dealt with the subject of medical research performed on inmates.
Which of the following is a feature of Connecticut's program?

    A. A fee schedule has been established which guarantees direct payment to inmate volunteers
    B. All inmates are equally eligible to participate in the program
    C. An inmate volunteer receives reasonable assurance that if he cooperates freely in the program he will receive additional *good time*
    D. Medical research programs enjoy the highest priority higher, for example, than vocational training programs

8. Inmate disorders must be dealt with instantly and decisively. Ringleaders in a disturbance must be

    A. punished immediately as an example to the other inmates
    B. identified immediately and then isolated
    C. punished by being placed in solitary confinement
    D. turned over to a psychologist or other clinician for treatment if they have been diagnosed as psychopathic

9. The Correction Law empowers the Department of Correction to establish a furlough program for certain sentenced inmates.
For an inmate to be eligible for consideration for this program, he must have served AT LEAST _____ months.

    A. two
    B. four
    C. six
    D. nine

Questions 10 - 13.

DIRECTIONS: Questions 10 through 13 are to be answered SOLELY on the basis of the following passage.

Traditional correctional institutions do not change or redirect the behavior of many of their inmates. Few of these establishments are equipped with adequate resources to treat the social and psychological handicaps of their wards. Too often, far removed ideolologically from the world to which its charges must return, the institution often compounds the problems its corrective mechanisms are intended to cure. Training school academic programs, for example, range from poor to totally inadequate and usually reinforce negative feelings toward future learning experiences. Vocational programs are frequently designed to benefit the institution without regard to the inmate, and the usual low-key common denominator treatment program scarcely begins to meet the needs of many offenders.

Most correctional institutions must mobilize their limited resources in time and talent for purposes other than the ever-present concern about runaways or escapes. No one could quarrel rationally with the need to safeguard the community and control the behavior of people who may be of danger to themselves or others. It is ridiculous and tragic, however, that an overstated security approach is still the rule for the bulk of our correctional population.

10. The passage states that inmates of traditional correctional institutions are LIKELY to

    A. develop belief in radical political ideologies
    B. experience conditions that produce no betterment
    C. give major attention to devising plans of escape
    D. desire vocational training unrelated to their individual potential

11. The passage indicates that traditional training school academic programs lead inmates to

    A. adjust to the institutional setting
    B. avoid later formal learning
    C. develop respect for the values of education
    D. request more practical, vocational training

12. The passage indicates that most traditional correctional institutions, because of their ideological distance from the realities of the outside world, are MOST LIKELY to

    A. ignore the safety of the outside community
    B. favor a minority of the inmate population
    C. lack properly motivated staff
    D. increase the problems of inmates

13. The passage states that the strong custodial function in most correctional institutions is MOST LIKELY to be

    A. accorded excessive emphasis
    B. aimed at incorrigible inmates only
    C. necessary to redirect inmate behavior
    D. resented by the outside community

Questions 14 - 16.

DIRECTIONS: Questions 14 through 16 are to be answered SOLELY on the basis of the following passage.

The most widely accepted argument in favor of the death penalty is that the threat of its infliction deters people from committing capital offenses. Of course, since human behavior can be influenced through fear, and since man tends to fear death, it is possible to use capital punishment as a deterrent. But the real question is whether individuals think of the death penalty before they act, and whether they are thereby deterred from committing crimes. If for the moment we assume that the death penalty does this to some extent, we must also grant that certain human traits limit its effectiveness as a deterrent. Man tends to be a creature of habit and emotion, and when his is handicapped by poverty, ignorance, and malnutrition, as criminals often are, he becomes notoriously shortsighted. Many violators of the law give little thought to the possibility of detection and apprehension, and often they do not even consider the penalty. Moreover, it appears that most people do not regulate their lives in terms of the pleasure and pain that may result from their acts.

Human nature is very complex. A criminal may fear punishment, but he may fear the anger and contempt of his companions or his family even more, and the fear of economic insecurity or exclusion from the group whose respect he cherishes may drive him to commit the most daring crimes. Besides, fear is not the only emotion that motivates man. Love, loyalty, ambition, greed, lust, anger, and resentment may steel him to face even death in the perpetration of crime, and impel him to devise the most ingenious methods to get what he wants and to avoid detection.

If the death penalty were surely, quickly, uniformly, publicly, and painfully inflicted, it undoubtedly would prevent many capital offenses that are being committed by those who do consider the punishment that they may receive for their crimes. But this is precisely the point. Certainly, the way in which the death penalty has been administered in the United States is not fitted to produce this result.

14. Of the following, the MOST appropriate title for the above passage is   14.____

    A. Capital Offenses in the United States
    B. The Death Penalty as a Deterrent
    C. Human Nature and Fear
    D. Emotion as a Cause of Crime

15. The above passage implies that the death penalty, as it has been administered in the United States,   15.____

    A. was too prompt and uniform to be effective
    B. deterred many criminals who considered the possible consequences of their actions
    C. prevented crimes primarily among habitual criminals
    D. failed to prevent the commission of many capital offenses

16. According to the above passage, many violators of the law are   16.____

    A. intensely concerned with the pleasure or pain that may result from their acts
    B. influenced primarily by economic factors
    C. not influenced by the opinions of their family or friends
    D. not seriously concerned with the possibility of apprehension

Questions 17 - 20.

DIRECTIONS: Questions 17 through 20 are to be answered SOLELY on the basis of the following passage:

The loss of control over the use of a drug — called addiction where there is both physical and psychological dependence, and habituation where there is psychological dependence without physical dependence — is, regardless of the particular drug involved, a disease. Both chronic alcoholism and narcotics addiction are usually recognized as diseases.

It is inappropriate to invoke the criminal process against persons who have lost control over the use of dangerous drugs solely because these persons are drug users. Once a person has lost control over his use of drugs, the existence of offenses such as drug use or simple possession will not deter his use. Having lost control, he cannot choose to conform his conduct to the requirements of the law by refraining from use. He is non-deterrable.

Admittedly, there may be times before a person loses control over his use of drugs when he did have a choice of whether to use or not to use, or to stop using. Because of this, punishing him for use or simple possession would not offend the principle that to be punishable conduct must be a result of free choice.

17. Of the following, the MOST suitable title for the above passage is

    A. Drug Addiction
    B. Drug Abuse and Punishment
    C. Habituation and the Criminal Process
    D. Preventing Drug Related Crime

18. According to the above passage, addiction and habituation are

    A. *identical* in meaning because both are diseases related to drug use
    B. *identical* in meaning because both involve dependence on drugs
    C. *similar* to the extent that both involve physical dependence on a drug
    D. *similar* to the extent that both involve psychological dependence on a drug

19. According to the above passage, punishing drug abusers would be justifiable ONLY if their behavior were

    A. elective
    B. non-deterrable
    C. chronic
    D. dangerous

20. According to the above passage, punishing a person for simple possession of drugs is

    A. appropriate under certain circumstances
    B. inappropriate because the person could not have acted otherwise
    C. necessary for the protection of society
    D. unfair because it penalizes past conduct

Questions 21 - 25.

DIRECTIONS: Questions 21 through 25 are to be answered SOLELY on the basis of the following notes and charts.

NOTES

Assume that correctional facilities in the town of Libertyville have recorded the number of individual inmate escape attempts, both successful and unsuccessful, for the year. This information is presented in Chart I.

Assume also that records were kept on the amount of time which elapsed between successful escapes by inmates and their recapture. This information is presented in Chart II.

ESCAPE ATTEMPTS BY INDIVIDUAL INMATES AT LIBERTYVILLE'S CORRECTIONAL FACILITIES, BY INMATE AGE GROUP

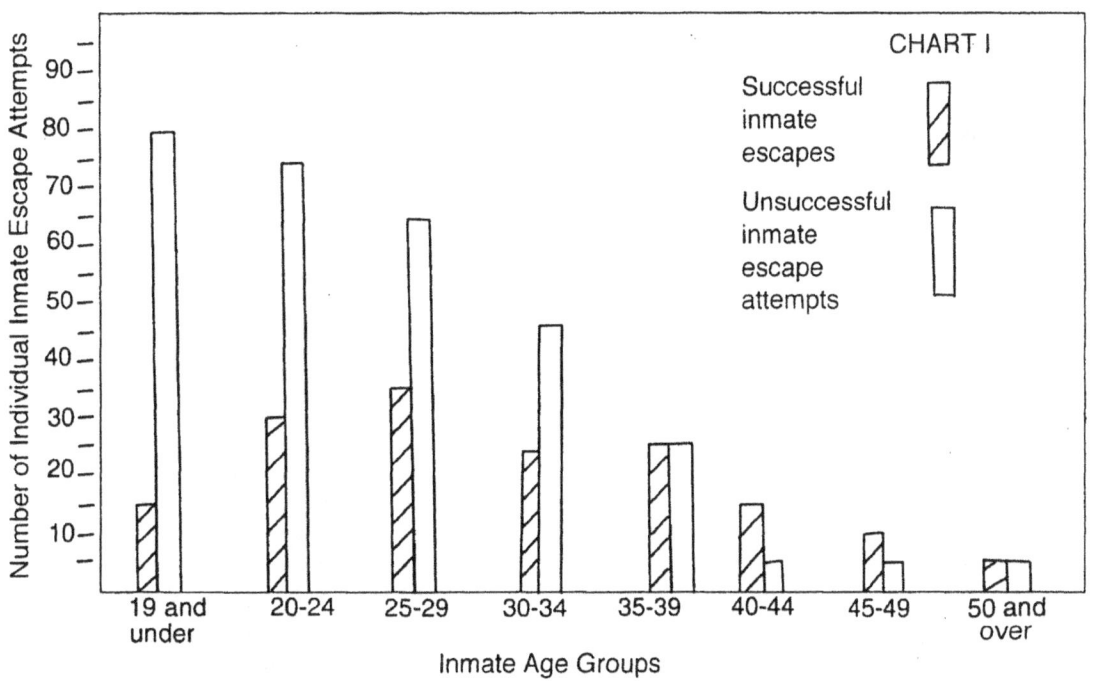

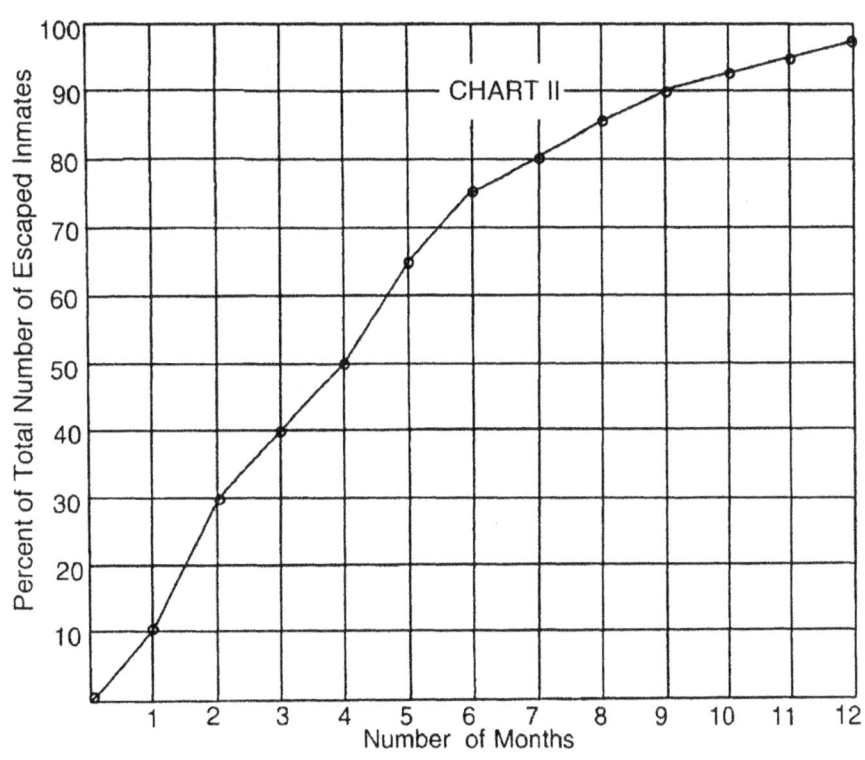

Time Period (in Months) Within Which Escaped Inmates Were Recaptured

21. Which of the following age groups shows a GREATER total number of escape attempts than the next youngest age group?

    A. 20-24   B. 25-29   C. 30-34   D. 35-39

22. Which of the following MOST NEARLY indicates the number of inmates who were recaptured within nine months of their escape?

    A. 90   B. 130   C. 145   D. 160

23. Based on the total number of escape attempts for each of the following age groups, which group had the HIGHEST percentage of successful escapes?

    A. 19 and under   B. 25-29
    C. 35-39   D. 45-49

24. An inmate who attempted to escape had GREATER than a 50% chance of

    A. *succeeding* if he was in the 25-29 group
    B. *failing* if he was in the 50 and over group
    C. *succeeding* if he was in the 40-44 group
    D. *failing* if he was in the 45-49 group

25. Which of the following statements concerning escaped inmates is NOT correct?

    A. Most of the inmates who escaped were under 30 years of age.
    B. One third of the escaped inmates were recaptured withing three months.
    C. Less than 10 per cent of the inmates who escaped were over 45 years of age.
    D. Seventy per cent of the escaped inmates were recaptured within six months.

KEY (CORRECT ANSWERS)

1. B		11. B	
2. D		12. D	
3. D		13. A	
4. A		14. B	
5. C		15. D	
6. B		16. D	
7. A		17. B	
8. B		18. D	
9. C		19. A	
10. B		20. A	

21. A
22. C
23. D
24. C
25. A

EXAMINATION SECTION
TEST 1

DIRECTIONS: Each question or incomplete statement is followed by several suggested answers or completions. Select the one that BEST answers the question or completes the statement. *PRINT THE LETTER OF THE CORRECT ANSWER IN THE SPACE AT THE RIGHT.*

1. Which of the following is MOST important in correcting unsatisfactory employee behavior?

    A. Assigning the employee to work closely with a more experienced employee
    B. Letting the employee know the most severe penalties for continued unsatisfactory behavior
    C. Getting the employee to admit that there is need for improvement in his behavior
    D. Conducting corrective interviews in groups, so that discussions can be uninhibited

2. Which of the following is the KEY to effective decision-making?

    A. Information analysis
    B. Operations research
    C. Planning
    D. Review

3. Scheduling the work of his group is one of the responsibilities of a supervisor.
The one of the following which is NOT a proper principle of work scheduling is

    A. assigning all the difficult jobs to the better workers
    B. keeping work related by time, space or function together
    C. making sure that all workers have sufficient work to achieve a meaningful day's work
    D. assigning a variety of work to each employee

4. There are four classic stages of teaching a job.
Of the following, the one which is NOT a classic stage of teaching a job is

    A. application or performance
    B. gradation or progression
    C. preparation or introduction
    D. presentation or demonstration

5. Which of the following statements INCORRECTLY describes the role of a supervisor? A (The) supervisor

    A. communicates to management the weaknesses in existing practices and recommends changes to meet actual conditions.
    B. carefully avoids critically appraising the work output of subordinates because to do so would adversely affect morale.
    C. accepts responsibility for the work output of subordinates.
    D. is the middle-man of an organization.

6. Trust, confidence, and respect by employees for their supervisors are built up by actions taken by the supervisor.
   Which one of the following supervisors conducts himself in a way that would PROBABLY be approved?
   Supervisor

   A. *A* is most comfortable when he is paternalistic. He freely gives advice on personal matters and is very interested in his employees' personal problems. He makes it a practice to chat frequently with his people on social subjects.
   B. *B* provides little supervision. He has formed a particularly close friendship with one of his employees who tells him about everything which goes on in the unit.
   C. *C* radiates self-confidence and positiveness. He takes no interest in employee problems. He dislikes employees who complain. Once he makes up his mind he does not change his views.
   D. *D* is willing to admit his personal inadequacies. He is willing to be frank about existing problems and existing working conditions. His philosophy is that to get you must give.

7. Which of the following statements BEST describes a view of what constitutes discipline?

   A. Discipline is a conditioner which rewards acceptable behavior and punishes unacceptable actions. It is a training procedure up to the point where diminishing results indicate further training is worthless.
   B. Discipline may be viewed as an internal regulating mechanism which constantly scans the various procedural alternatives available in the work situation. The selection of less than the perfect solution should be followed promptly by corrective action.
   C. Discipline may best be described as a subjective procedure. Discipline should not be undertaken without consultation with one's superiors.
   D. Plainly described, discipline is a procedure for insuring that departmental rules and regulations are carried out to the letter.

8. With respect to the training function, which of the following CORRECTLY states the position?

   A. Employee training can be handled very effectively as part of the supervisor-supervised relationship with the supervisor doing the training.
   B. On-the-job training can never by as effective as classroom training because employee supervisors are generally not conscientious listeners.
   C. Supervisors occasionally make effective trainers provided that they receive formal instruction in training techniques and can discipline themselves not to look down upon those who require training.
   D. The major point to be made in favor of training by supervisor is that such training gives supervisors an opportunity to review their own procedures.

9. Assume that a situation arises in your department which will require a considerable amount of overtime work which will by paid for in cash or in time off at the employee's option. One employee has financial problems and wants all the overtime he can get, another states he can work late only two days a week because of social plans, a third employee who is unmarried does not want to work overtime. The principle to be kept in mind in assigning employees to work overtime is that

A. a discreet assessment must be made of each individual's situation, with overtime being assigned to those in greatest need
B. if a man cannot work overtime in an agency responsible for the administration of justice he belongs in another job
C. it is a poor supervisory practice to ask an employee to work overtime when he does not wish to do so, so long as there is another employee willing to report for duty
D. Whenever overtime may be compensated for in cash, the supervisor should view this as an additional opportunity to reward those who by their loyalty and efficiency have earned the right to overtime work

10. The lecture method of training employees is

    A. of considerable value in refresher training but otherwise has more disadvantages than advantages
    B. probably the most valuable technique of teaching provided that the lecturer has a dynamic rapid-fire method of presenting the material
    C. suitable only for training entry-level employees
    D. a one-way communication process that does not attempt to evaluate whether the student understands the lecture

11. Assume that a certain agency makes it a practice to penalize an employee who is late in reporting for duty. If he is late a second time in a particular month his penalty is more severe. If he is late a third time in the month, the penalty is still more severe.
    An employee will USUALLY view this type of agency policy of increasing penalties as

    A. *bad*, fairness requires that there should be no penalty the first time an employee is guilty of an infraction
    B. *bad*, the commission of an infraction by an employee is usually unintentional
    C. *good*, more severe sanctions for repeated infractions are just
    D. *good*, sanctions are nearly always less severe than the circumstances warrant

12. The view on employee morale is that

    A. a supervisor develops the highest state of employee morale by the "carrot and stick" philosophy of rewarding good behavior and punishing bad behavior
    B. every person's morale is low in a unit where the chuckling loafer gets paid as much as the disgruntled high-pressure producer
    C. it is necessary to constantly maintain an equilibrium within the organization in which all members of the work group can obtain satisfaction
    D. high morale is rarely, if ever, possible in positions involving the administration of justice because the client population tends to be resistive and resentful

13. A characteristic of the EFFECTIVE leader-supervisor is

    A. a desire to become thoroughly familiar with the latest studies in his field
    B. a willingness to engage in risk-taking behavior
    C. complete familiarity with his departmental rules and regulations
    D. the courage to mete out swift punishment for infractions

14. Effective communication requires a *climate of acceptance.*
In order to achieve this *climate of acceptance,* the supervisor should

    A. cheerfully accept the blame for errors innocently made by subordinates
    B. conduct himself in a way which leads his subordinates to regard him as trustworthy
    C. maintain a personal notebook in which he keeps a record of the orders he has issued
    D. never issue an order without giving a supporting reason for the order

15. As a supervisor, you notice that one of your older correction officers who is in charge of a work detail is lackadaisical in searching inmates for contraband and only *brushes* inmates over lightly. You mention this in passing to him but he continues in this practice. You should

    A. ask the officer to search the inmates again and again until you are satisfied that the correction officer has learned his lesson
    B. promptly refer the matter to your superior officer for appropriate disciplinary action
    C. recognize that this officer cannot be retrained and should be assigned to duties that do not involve searching inmates
    D. re-search the inmates in the detail yourself even if this proves embarrassing to the officer

16. There are certain tried and tested principles and techniques which the correctional officer must master if he is to be successful in supervising incarcerated offenders. One of these principles is: A correction officer should not be too anxious to reveal completely to inmates what he knows and thinks.
Which of the following is a reason for applying this principle?

    A. A correction officer should discipline himself to think in terms of action rather than in terms of concepts.
    B. An inmate's action is often influenced favorably when he fears the unknown.
    C. Inmate feelings of self-respect are enhanced if they believe they know something the correction officer does not know.
    D. To the greatest extent possible, a correction officer should speak to inmates only when he is spoken to.

17. Inmates generally find their place in some group within the institution. A certain correction officer makes it a practice to find out as much as he can about such groups and the reasons for changes in their composition. The correction officer's practice in this regard is considered to be

    A. *bad*, a correctional officer who develops a reputation for not minding his own business will be taken as a hostage in the event of a disturbance
    B. *bad*, within institutional rules, an inmate has as much right to a personal social life as anyone else
    C. *good*, institutional security may depend upon such observation
    D. *good*, most inmates are appreciative when correction officers show a personal interest in their activities

18. Assume that an inmate is inclined to be grouchy and disagreeable on a certain day due to a feeling of confinement. The correction officer in charge of the inmate decides to leave the inmate temporarily alone but observing his actions.
The correction officer's action is

A. *improper,* the correction officer should have a sympathetic talk with the inmate
B. *improper,* the duties of a correction officer should not vary according to each inmate's moods
C. *proper,* ordering an inmate to "snap out of it" in such a case is likely to precipitate a precipitate a large-scale disturbance
D. *proper,* such moods occur more or less frequently with every inmate

19. Assume that an emotionally disturbed inmate is threatening to become violent. The correction officer who observes this should

    A. address the inmate in a humorous vein, pointing out that the inmate is making himself appear ridiculous
    B. deal with the inmate in a firm, unemotional way, and if this does not work he should summon assistance
    C. remain perfectly still, being certain to keep his hands visible to the inmate
    D. tell the inmate in a positive way that he is faking and quickly frisk the inmate to make certain that he does not have a weapon with which he can harm others or himself.

20. Assume that an educated, successful individual has just been Assume that an educated, successful individual has just been convicted for a sex crime. He tells you in a calm and rational manner that the way for him to solve his problem is to commit suicide. A moment later he laughs and assures you that he was only kidding.
    You should

    A. immediately ask the inmate if he would care to discuss the matter in greater detail with your own superior officer
    B. advise him that sex crimes are no longer viewed as seriously as they were at one time
    C. see to it that this matter is promptly referred to the clinical staff and that the inmate is kept under close surveillance
    D. watch this inmate carefully for the onset of symptoms of depression

21. Assume that a recently arrested person has a severe attack of epilepsy. He blacked out at first, becomes stiff, and has difficulty breathing. This is followed by severe muscle twitching and shaking of the body. His mouth is firmly closed. You summon medical assistance but you have reason to believe that it will be ten to fifteen minutes before help arrives.
    Emergency handling of an epileptic convulsion involves

    A. the understanding that one must let the spell run its course
    B. forcibly prying the mouth open to insert a tongue depressor or if not available a handkerchief or even one of the victim's socks
    C. talking to the victim in a soothing manner, repeatedly assuring him that help will arrive shortly
    D. the prevention of shock by vigorously massaging the area directly above the heart

22. If a correction officer would successfully influence the conduct of inmates, he MUST

    A. be prepared to frankly discuss charges which may be pending against an inmate
    B. gracefully accept his own emotional weaknesses as a means of better understanding inmate behavior
    C. identify at an emotional level with the personality problems of the inmates
    D. view the inmate as a potentially well-adjusted individual

23. A monthly training bulletin lists certain conditions as indicators of an impending riot. Which one of the following is NOT listed as such an indicator?
    The number of

    A. fights within groups or between groups increases
    B. inmates who act friendly toward custodial officers increases
    C. inmates who request change in assignments increases
    D. violations of institutional rules and regulations increases

24. Which one of the following statements regarding the use of firearms is CORRECT?

    A. Check and test the safety catch of your weapon at least twice in any twenty-four-hour period.
    B. Clean and oil your weapon at least once a week whether or not it has been used.
    C. Never allow your weapon to be used by another correction officer.
    D. Never point your weapon, whether loaded or unloaded, at anyone unless you mean to shoot.

25. A correction officer is expected to see and report unusual situations to his superior. He should use all of his senses.
    Which one of the following statements regarding the use of sight by a correction officer is CORRECT?
    The officer should

    A. keep his eyes constantly on inmates in his charge since observation is an effective medium for control and custody.
    B. look just over the inmates' heads since this will keep inmates from becoming nervous while the officer's peripheral vision takes in that which is important.
    C. not allow his eyes to rest on any one inmate since that is a certain method for provoking hostility.
    D. train himself so that his eyes concentrate on the hands of inmates since information gained from looking at inmates faces is usually unreliable.

KEY (CORRECT ANSWERS)

1. C
2. D
3. A
4. B
5. B

6. D
7. A
8. A
9. C
10. D

11. C
12. C
13. B
14. B
15. D

16. B
17. C
18. D
19. B
20. C

21. A
22. D
23. B
24. D
25. A

TEST 2

DIRECTIONS: Each question or incomplete statement is followed by several suggested answers or completions. Select the one that BEST answers the question or completes the statement. *PRINT THE LETTER OF THE CORRECT ANSWER IN THE SPACE AT THE RIGHT.*

1. The FUNDAMENTAL responsibility of prison management is the
    A. secure custody and control of prisoners
    B. development of work programs for prisoners
    C. training of prisoners
    D. classification of prisoners

    1.____

2. The number of counts made in a 24-hour period should be
    A. 1   B. 4   C. 6   D. 8

    2.____

3. Medium security classification means an inmate
    A. cannot work outside the regular enclosure
    B. is not eligible for dormitory housing
    C. can work outside the regular enclosure under supervision
    D. may be eligible for work release

    3.____

4. The MOST frequent violation of the fundamentals of key control is that of the officer
    A. permitting the wrong inmate to handle keys
    B. entering a cell block where inmates are confined with keys to outer doors
    C. failing to give a receipt for his keys
    D. taking his keys home

    4.____

5. It is wrong for the correction officer, while making a count, to
    A. concentrate only on the count as the round is made
    B. see flesh or movement before recording inmate as counted
    C. count in a dormitory or an open type unit by himself
    D. list one part of a unit, when completed, on a temporary count sheet

    5.____

6. Which of the following guidelines is LEAST appropriate for a key control system in a correctional institution?
    A. All keys should be issued from a central location such as the institution control room.
    B. Officers should not be permitted to withdraw keys unless they give receipts for the keys.
    C. The key control center should have at all times at least one duplicate set for each bunch of keys.
    D. Only reliable prisoners such as trustees should be permitted to handle keys.

    6.____

7. Following are three statements concerning weapons and ammunition in correctional institutions that MIGHT BE correct:
   I. Weapons should generally be stored in a secure area inside the institution.
   II. Shipments of weapons or ammunition coming into institutions should be plainly labeled.
   III. The habitual use of weapons in close proximity to prisoners is an example of false security.

   Which of the following choices lists *all* of the above statements that ARE generally correct?

   A. I and II, but not III
   B. I and III, but not II
   C. II and III, but not I
   D. I, II, and III

8. Under the system which is presently the most widely used method of industrial employment for prisoners, it would be CORRECT to state that

   A. the sale of prison-made goods is restricted to departments and institutions of the state and its political subdivisions
   B. prisoners are removed from institutions to engage in outside work, with the employer paying the state a designated sum for the services of the prisoners
   C. the state functions in the role of manufacturer and assumes the expense of producing prison-made goods for a virtually unrestricted market
   D. manufacturers contract with states for the products made by prisoners, supervise the working inmates, and market the finished products

9. Which of the following statements concerning the relationship between custody and rehabilitative programs is INCORRECT?

   A. Services and facilities for rehabilitative treatment can operate effectively only in a climate where control is constant.
   B. Positive programs of inmate activities generally weaken the effectiveness of security measures.
   C. Rehabilitative services must be correlated with a system of sound custody, security, and control of inmates.
   D. Security and control procedures will produce maximum results when they are implemented in a manner which gains the cooperation of the majority of inmates.

10. The essential features of good organizational structure for an institution for adult prisoners should include all of the following EXCEPT

    A. a constructive system of communication with inmates
    B. a program of personnel development for correctional staff including the classification of positions and in-service training
    C. separate administrative controls for the personnel, inmates, and programs of the institution
    D. a system for developing constructive community relationships

11. The classification process consists of organized procedures by which diagnosis, treatment planning, and the general treatment program are coordinated.
    The classification process should be focused on

    A. the security of the institution
    B. programs of treatment
    C. the individual inmate
    D. specialized facilities

12. Which of the following is MOST likely to contribute to the effectiveness of the classification process?

    A. Consideration of data obtained through the observations of inmates by custodial officers
    B. Commitment of prisoners by the courts to specified institutions
    C. Inspection of security facilities on a regular basis
    D. Uniformity of program details among various facilities

13. Community correctional institutions have been proposed as an alternative to jails for short-term misdemeanor offenders. Such facilities would be reception-diagnostic and treatment centers.
    The MINIMUM that these community correctional institutions can do for prisoners serving short sentences is to

    A. offer workshops and training in job skills
    B. provide psychological and educational assistance to each individual
    C. restore dislocated persons to community or family care
    D. eliminate as much as possible the degrading influence of incarceration

14. The use, where possible, of consolidated jails serving several jurisdictions has been recommended in lieu of individual local facilities.
    Of the following, the MAJOR advantage of consolidated jails is that

    A. a more effective correctional program can be offered when funds and other resources are pooled
    B. the population of local jails is reduced to more manageable proportions
    C. special institutions such as farms, camps, and workhouses can develop their separate treatment methods
    D. community acceptance is more easily obtained for one large facility than for several smaller ones

15. Secondary prevention is considered by some correctional authorities to be a promising method of protecting society against crime.
    Of the following, secondary prevention refers PRINCIPALLY to the

    A. wider use of probation as an alternative to commitment for offenders
    B. prevention of repeated crime through the correctional training and treatment of offenders
    C. post-institutional treatment of inmates under parole supervision
    D. establishment of community-centered correctional residence for parolees

16. It is generally accepted in the correctional field that society is best protected when a very high percentage of all releases are by parole.
    The is TRUE *primarily* because

    A. it costs much less to handle inmates on parole than to incarcerate them in institutions
    B. indeterminate sentences give correctional administrators maximum flexibility
    C. the bad risks who need it most will be under supervision after release
    D. it is relatively easy to determine what constitutes success or failure on parole

17. Jails should be used to detain *only* prisoners awaiting

    A. court action
    B. court action and those few short sentence prisoners who require maximum security
    C. court action and most short-sentence prisoners
    D. court action, short-sentence prisoners, and a few longer-sentence prisoners who must be near community facilities

18. Which of the following statements regarding standards for measuring the effectiveness of correctional institutions is NOT correct?

    A. The number of violations by parolees and the frequency of escapes from prison are easily tabulated but are unreliable indices.
    B. The calculation of correctional effectiveness is a problem in social engineering whose solution lies in the application of scientific method of correctional data.
    C. Increasingly, the criterion of success or failure of correctional institutions is recidivism.
    D. Although it is concerned with all aspects of behavior, corrections has only recently developed universally accepted standards for evaluating the work of the members.

19. Probation may be defined as a SENTENCE, as an ORGANIZATION, or as a PROCESS. The capitalized terms in the statement are described by the following three statements:
    I.   A service agency designed to assist the court and to execute certain services in the administration of criminal justice
    II. A judicial disposition which establishes the defendant's legal status
    III. The pre-sentence investigation for the court and the supervision of persons in the community

    Which of the following choices correctly matches the numbered statements and the italicized terms they define?

    A. I-process;   II-organization;   III-sentence
    B. I-organization; II-sentence;   III-process
    C. I-process;   II-sentence;   III-organization
    D. I-organization; II-process;   III-sentence

20. Many prison administrators now recognize a mutuality of interests between corrections and certain community agencies.
    This mutuality of interests is based PRIMARILY on the fact that

    A. prison officials today understand the importance of good public relations
    B. inmates are now aware of the many community-based programs that are available to them
    C. community agencies can provide assistance in terminating an offender's criminal career
    D. probation and parole officials are making greater use of community agencies than in the past

21. There are two basic general causes of riots and disturbances in correctional institutions which cannot be directly attributed to institutional variables within the control of institutional administrators.
    These GENERAL causes are:

    A. a lack of courage on the part of some elected officials which prevents the prompt quelling of riots and a desire on the part of the communications media to publicize unfounded charges by inmates
    B. A rapidly rising standard of living to which few can aspire and an irresponsible press and television which financially profits from violence
    C. The spirit of rebellion in today's youth and the failure of parents to take an interest in the welfare of either their adolescent or pre-adolescent children
    D. The unnatural nature of the environment in a correctional institution and the antisocial characteristics of inmates

22. In a correctional institution, discord between administrative and line personnel is MOST likely to

    A. diminish the effectiveness of treatment programs and increase the level of emotional stress and discontent among the inmate population
    B. increase considerably the funds for certain types of treatment programs while sharply reducing the funds available for treatment programs which are unpopular with inmate leaders
    C. temporarily raise the morale of the inmate population which soon fails precipitously as inmates become aware that the more devious of their number are plotting to use this situation as a means of instigating violence
    D. usually be viewed by the inmate population as an opportunity to play one group off against the other which, in effect, surrenders the operation of the institution to the inmate population

23. A positive program of maintaining discipline is essential in preventing unrest or disturbances.
    A good disciplinary program is one that

    A. is based on the use of disciplinary committees to punish all infractions of the rules
    B. does not include punishment for violations of the rules except in extreme cases
    C. maintains order with minimal friction, using punishment in a constructive manner
    D. uses administrative segregation as the basic method for controlling inmates

24. Which of the following statements concerning riots and disturbances in correctional institutions is CORRECT?

    A. A system which provides for both formal and informal communications between staff and inmates is the best means for preventing riots and disturbances.
    B. Research studies have identified a set of causes which will always precipitate a riot.
    C. Sudden or unexpected changes in institutional routines or policies may result in a major stabilization.
    D. The best means for preventing riots is to have an effective informant system.

25. Projects in correctional institutions such as Jaycees, Alcoholics Anonymous and group-study clubs have been found to 25.____

    A. insure the success of inmates in adapting to the institutional environment
    B. serve exclusively as manipulative devices used by inmates
    C. be of little or no value, either to inmates or to institutional staff
    D. be useful as. communicative devices between inmates and officials when they are well-defined and well-supervised

KEY (CORRECT ANSWERS)

1.	A	11.	C
2.	B	12.	A
3.	C	13.	D
4.	B	14.	A
5.	C	15.	B
6.	D	16.	C
7.	C	17.	B
8.	A	18.	D
9.	B	19.	B
10.	C	20.	C

21. D
22. A
23. C
24. A
25. D

EXAMINATION SECTION
TEST 1

DIRECTIONS: Each question or incomplete statement is followed by several suggested answers or completions. Select the one that BEST answers the question or completes the statement. *PRINT THE LETTER OF THE CORRECT ANSWER IN THE SPACE AT THE RIGHT.*

1. The MOST accurate statement concerning inmate living quarters is: The

    A. open dormitory encourages harmonious group relations and is ordinarily the best approach
    B. open dormitory is usually preferred by inmates who find difficulty in establishing social relationships since it gives them a wider area from which to form close friendships
    C. private room with no window but with a barred cell door facing a corridor is the best approach since the existence of a window fosters unconscious suicidal tendencies
    D. private room with outside window establishes *individuality and territory* and is considered the best approach

1.____

2. If a group of rioting inmates demands that they negotiate directly with the Governor of the state, the request should PROBABLY be

    A. *denied;* leading political figures can always be depended upon to make false or unworkable promises in order to get credit for ending the riot
    B. *denied;* the granting of such a request lends encouragement to other inmates of other institutions to repeat the same show on another stage
    C. *granted;* inmates who do not receive satisfaction will torture hostages and destroy property
    D. *granted;* the public regrettably has a greater confidence in the ability of a governor to handle a riot than in the abilities of correction officials

2.____

3. Assume that you are a superior. An inmate comes to you with a request arising out of a grievance he has which he believes to be legitimate. You can see that the inmate is making a request which is important to him. You consider the inmate's request carefully and decide that you cannot grant the inmate's request.
It would be BEST for you to

    A. give the inmate a firm *no* answer and your reason for doing so
    B. grant the inmate's request because of its importance but point out to him that there were very good reasons for not granting the request
    C. tell the inmate that his request is an important one and you will let him know in the not too distant future whether his request can be granted
    D. tell the inmate that there are two sides to his request and that you will ask the Deputy Warden to frame a written response to the inmate

3.____

4. Assume that you are a superior and that the early warning signs of an inmate disturbance are present in your institution. One of the officers you supervise behaves in a very nervous, insecure way in the presence of inmates. You try to encourage the officer to behave in a confident manner but the officer is unable to do so.
In the circumstances, it would probably be BEST to

4.____

A. hold a brief meeting with the other line officers who comprise your staff and ask for suggestions on dealing with the officer
B. order the officer to straighten up or face disciplinary charges
C. recommend that the officer be temporarily assigned to a less sensitive area
D. shock the officer into proper behavior by asking him if he intends to turn *yellow* should trouble break out

5. There is a strong disagreement among correctional administrators concerning the use of inmate councils.
The MOST feasible approach concerning the use of inmate councils is generally the

   A. elimination of inmate advisory groups, since membership in such a group gives the inmate member an opportunity to exploit other inmate members
   B. formation of inmate advisory groups to deal with particular problems, with such groups dissolving as soon as the problem is resolved
   C. popular election by inmates of an inmate advisory group to meet at frequent periodic intervals
   D. taking of formal surveys by supervisory correction personnel to determine inmate attitudes

6. Which of the following may spark a prison riot or major prison disturbance?

   A. Absence of clearly defined and easily understood rules and regulations
   B. Indecisive actions on legitimate inmate grievances
   C. Poor communications
   D. All of the above

7. Which of the following is NOT true?

   A. A disproportionate share of individuals who are prone to violent behavior are to be found in correctional institutions.
   B. Inmates have high self-esteem and are fully committed to the major goal of making large sums of money.
   C. Inmates are more apt to be mentally deficient than persons who are not in correctional institutions.
   D. Inmates are frequently the product of broken homes, are unskilled, and have unstable work records.

8. Of the following, the MOST correct statement is:
Riots

   A. are caused by a conscious desire to bring about revolutionary improvements in the American social system and to put an end to the devaluation of certain elements of the population by those who are in positions of power
   B. come about because institutional life is monotonous and because inmates feel a sense of being hopelessly oppressed and stripped of all human dignity
   C. are complex phenomena for which simple explanations do not in reality exist
   D. are violent acts contrary to law and are proof positive of the moral deterioration of middle-class America

9. Assume that you have made an informal count of a small inmate work crew assigned to a small area on a site that has never known an escape. There is doubt in your mind as to the correctness of your count.
   Your BEST reaction is that

   A. there is no cause for immediate alarm, since only formal crew counts are recorded
   B. you should first count the crew again
   C. you should waste no time in reporting an inmate missing and then, after the report is made, count the crew again
   D. you should ask the crew whether one of the inmates is missing

10. The BASIC function of a correctional institution is

    A. to operate at maximum efficiency
    B. to make certain that every department understands that teamwork is vital and that all departments are important
    C. the protection of society and the rehabilitation of the inmates
    D. the recognition that correctional institutions face a more difficult problem than at any time in the history of our country

11. It is sometimes necessary for a correction officer to order an inmate to do something the officer knows the inmate will not like to do.
    In these circumstances, the following is the recommended BEST procedure:

    A. Convince the inmate of the merit of your order before the inmate carries it out
    B. Do not insist upon immediate compliance with the order but give the inmate time to come to the realization that it is best to comply with an officer's order
    C. If faced with total refusal, restructure the order and emphasize a different aspect of the original order
    D. Make sure that the order is carried out completely

12. The use of food for payment of work or for special privileges has no justification and such practice should never be permitted and will very likely get completely out of control and develop a usage of large amounts of luxury goods.
    Which one of the following would be an EXCEPTION to the preceding passage?

    A. The giving of large portions of meat to those who are given arduous work assignments
    B. An officer who gives extra portions of food to those inmates who have been helpful to the officer during the day
    C. The giving of an extra large piece of pastry by a kitchen helper to an officer while on duty in the dining hall
    D. An officer who allows the kitchen help to keep leftovers which are storable

13. The MAJOR purpose of a perimeter search is to

    A. assure that all cell blocks are secure
    B. discover whether any tools have been taken from the work area
    C. keep illegal items from being passed among the inmates while in open courtyards
    D. make sure contraband doesn't enter from the outside

14. A major point of emphasis in the instruction of a correction officer concerns security and the causes of breach of security.
Experience has shown that MOST escapes are traceable directly to

   A. relatives who smuggle escape instruments to inmates
   B. officers who smuggle contraband to inmates
   C. the haphazard handling of keys and tools
   D. the lack of knowledge among inmates as to the possible consequences of escape

15. Reception centers have been established in several of the larger states.
The BASIC idea behind the reception centers is that

   A. before an offender has been found guilty in court, a sound orientation program should be instituted designed to facilitate good adjustment to healthy social life
   B. before an offender has been found guilty in court, the decision as to the value of lenient treatment should be decided by specialists in the correctional and rehabilitation fields
   C. after an offender has been found guilty in court, the decision as to the place and method of treatment should be decided by specialists in the correction field
   D. after an offender has been found guilty in court, immediate psychiatric examination should determine the inmate's attitude toward work and his future vocational program

16. The key to the successful operation of a classification program in a prison institution is the

   A. professional qualifications of the psychiatrist and social worker
   B. support and leadership given by the head of the institution
   C. careful application of the techniques and purposes of scientific classification
   D. willing participation of the hardened inmates

17. Classification, as the term is generally used in correctional work, is PRIMARILY

   A. a method that will assure coordination in diagnosis, training, and treatment of prison inmates
   B. in itself diagnosis, training, and treatment of prison inmates
   C. integration of like or similar groups of offenders into the general inmate population
   D. the labeling of prison inmates in different mental or attitudinal categories or types and the measurement of willingness to work

18. A study of the Federal prison system has compared the yearly average number of escapes per thousand inmates for the four years BEFORE and AFTER their classification program was established.
This comparison shows that the rate of escapes per year

   A. was much higher before classification
   B. is unknown because no such study has ever been officially approved
   C. was much lower after classification
   D. was about the same before and after classification

19. All studies of parole failures have shown that, of the following, the highest percentage of violations occur after the inmate has been released

    A. six months
    B. one month
    C. one week
    D. 12-14 months

20. Many correctional administrators believe that any institution operating as a single unit becomes increasingly inefficient and unsafe as its inmate population exceeds a critical figure. This critical figure can be enlarged by breaking up the institution into several smaller units, but still operating as a single administrative unit, or by locating two or more separate institutions on the same site.
    In building new facilities or splitting older institutions into more manageable small units, it is considered unwise for the number of inmates to be included in any one unit to exceed

    A. 1200   B. 1000   C. 50   D. 600

21. As a group, youthful offenders are _____ susceptible to positive treatment efforts than juvenile delinquents _____.

    A. *less;* or adult criminals
    B. *more;* or adult criminals
    C. *more;* but they are not as susceptible to positive treatment efforts as adult criminals
    D. *less;* but they are more susceptible to positive treatment efforts than adult criminals

22. Perhaps the young person who becomes legally defined as an offender has developed and become *socialized* in a milieu more characterized by anti-social than social customs and standards. His inability to control himself according to the requirements of the larger social order then signifies commitment to an unacceptable code of conduct rather than psychological aberration.
    An implication of the foregoing is that

    A. a young offender in an institutional setting will accept the guidance of fellow inmates and not that of treatment or custodial personnel
    B. where a youthful offender lacks self-control his behavior toward his associates is bound to be assaultive
    C. the use of narcotics or *hard* drugs may assist the individual to escape from people and problems
    D. the young offender may behave according to the standards of his friends and neighbors

23. There are three major means by which a conviction may be set aside after the ordinary statutory channels of appeal are closed.
    Which one of the following is NOT such a major means?

    A. Parole
    B. Habeas corpus
    C. Pardon
    D. Coram nobis

24. Which of the following types of housing is deemed preferable for female inmates?

    A. Cottage type
    B. Dormitory type
    C. One inmate per cell
    D. Three inmates per cell

25. Regarding library services, which of the following is recommended?

    A. Inmates should be encouraged to ask friends, relatives, and charitable organizations to contribute funds for the operation of the institutional library.
    B. Since most inmates are functional illiterates, at least ten comic books per inmate should be purchased for the institutional library.
    C. The requirement of a male librarian in all-male institutions should be waived since experience has proved that women are highly efficient and effective serving as librarians in all-male institutions.
    D. To discourage the planning of disturbances, inmates should not be permitted to read books in the library.

26. Which of the following measures is deemed to be advisable in establishing property control standards for inmates entering prison?

    A. An inmate's valuables should be itemized and sealed in a clear plastic bag.
    B. Inmates should be permitted to retain on their persons their social security cards, watches, and small quantities of postage stamps.
    C. Inmates who handle inmates' personal property should be carefully selected for their qualities of trustworthiness.
    D. Jewelry taken from inmates at time of incarceration should be carefully described with such words as gold, silver, diamond, or ruby to avoid the possibility of substitution.

27. Emergency doors must be provided into housing and to the areas where prisoners are congregated.
    All housing units should have an emergency entrance door with a lock opening on the _____ only and the door made to swing _____ only.

    A. inside; inward   B. inside; outward
    C. outside; inward   D. outside; outward

28. Which of the following does NOT represent the view of authorities regarding the use of tear gas?

    A. A limitation on using gas inside a building is the danger of getting a concentration which is too dense.
    B. It is economically sound to keep large quantities of gas munitions on hand due to the economies of large scale purchasing.
    C. The threat and availability of gas at the scene of a disturbance has probably halted more incipient disorders than its actual use.
    D. The use of tear gas in suppressing disturbances is more humane than bullets.

29. To schedule an official count at or near the time of officer shift changes is USUALLY found to be a

    A. *bad* practice since officers corning on duty resent being held up while a previous shift makes its count
    B. *bad* practice since officers responsible for the count are too easily distracted
    C. *good* practice since accuracy in the count is assured and interference with inmate activities is avoided
    D. *good* practice since a large number of officers will be on hand if discrepancies in the count are found

30. More disturbances have originated or culminated in the _____ areas than any other area.
    Which of the following words, when inserted in the blank space, would MOST accurately complete the statement?

    A. dining
    B. housing
    C. recreational
    D. work

31. According to a recent handbook on how to recognize and handle abnormal people, the BEST way, generally, to handle a disturbed, potentially violent person is to

    A. display any physical restraint that is readily available and calmly but firmly tell the inmate that the restraint will be employed unless he apologizes for his behavior
    B. try to talk to him and find out what is bothering him, since this tends to gain his confidence
    C. tell him whatever he wants to hear since the deception of an abnormal individual is necessary for his own protection
    D. be as self-confident and assured as possible since an easy approach will appear as a sign of weakness to a deranged mind

32. Assume that you are explaining a procedure to a visitor to an inmate in an institution, but the visitor does not seem to quite understand what you are saying. This lack of understanding has occurred occasionally in the past with other visitors. A language barrier does not appear to be the problem.
    According to a training bulletin issued by the City Department of Correction, the BEST way, generally, to handle this type of situation is to

    A. carefully use appropriately colorful language, since the display of colorful words will likely stimulate the visitor to an understanding of your instructions
    B. gently question the visitor's inborn communications capacity, since a little kidding often goes a long way to bridge a communications gap
    C. slowly increase a show of legitimate authority, since a little authority goes a long way in expediting matters with insecure persons
    D. find out what the visitor does not understand, since this may provide a clue as to improvements in your explanation

Questions 33-42.

DIRECTIONS: Questions 33 through 42 consist of two statements, based on the current Rules and Regulations and Manual of Procedure, Department of Correction.
If BOTH statements are correct, mark your answer A.
If NEITHER statement is correct, mark your answer B.
If Statement I ONLY is correct, but NOT Statement II, mark your answer C.
If Statement II ONLY is correct, but NOT Statement I, mark your answer D.

33. I. In the event of an inmate's death in any institution of the Correction Department, four people only shall be immediately notified in the following order: the institutional physician, the police precinct having jurisdiction, the Commissioner of Correction, and the Director of Operations.

    II. In the event of an attempted suicide by an inmate in his cell, the correction officer who first observes the incident shall immediately administer first aid. In the event that the inmate does not respond to first aid, the correction officer shall notify a superior officer or another correction officer in the vicinity to assist in the administration of first aid.

34. I. Upon the escape of an inmate, if the escapee is a member of a work gang, the officer in charge shall immediately line up all the inmates and, as expeditiously as possible, communicate with his superior officer.

    II. A correction officer shall be constantly alert while on duty, observing everything that takes place on his post within his sight or hearing, and shall periodically patrol his post during his tour of duty.

35. I. Whenever an inmate receives a written communication from a duly accredited reporter requesting permission to interview him, the inmate, if he wishes to be interviewed, shall submit such information in writing to the head of the institution.

    II. The following shall be the only types of punishment administered: reprimand; loss of one or more privileges, temporarily or permanently; loss of part or all good time; punitive segregation; restricted diets.

36. I. A correction officer in charge of any area within an institution shall check all bars, locks, windows, doors, and other security facilities on his post at least twice during his tour of duty for evidence that they are in good condition and have not been tampered with.

    II. When it is deemed necessary at any time to search the person of any employee on duty, such search shall be made by a captain or other superior officer. Refusal of any employee to be searched shall constitute grounds for disciplinary action.

37. I. Whenever prisoners are received from departmental and police vans, they must be searched and counted as soon as possible.

    II. The following categories of inmates shall not be assigned as sentenced help:
    a. Drug Addicts or Drug Offenders
    b. Gambling Law Violators

38. I. A correction officer assigned to court detention pens shall each day check the court calendar with the names of the prisoners sent from the various institutions.

    II. A captain shall call the attention of the assistant deputy warden to all matters of importance within the institution. The assistant deputy warden shall, in turn, call these matters of importance to the attention of the head of institution, the relieving assistant deputy warden, and the relieving captain.

39. I. In the event that any employee is made captive by prisoners, all orders issued by him during his captivity shall have full force and effect, except as pertaining to inmates.

    II. There shall be no restrictions as to correspondents, nor to the number of letters an inmate of any institution may receive as incoming mail or send out as outgoing mail.

40. I. No cell, tier, floor, or dormitory assignment of inmates, or changes in such assignments, shall be made without the authorization of a captain or other superior officer.
    II. Whenever a correction officer receives information from any source which directly or indirectly involves the security of any institution, he shall immediately notify the head of his institution or division.

41. I. A designated captain shall be responsible for the daily accounting of all firearms and protective equipment assigned to an institution or division.
    II. Whenever an inmate commits an infraction of discipline important enough to necessitate action, the captain or other superior officer on duty in the institution shall, as soon as practicable, but no later than the same day, investigate the complaint and, if in his judgment the facts warrant, he will place the inmate in punishment status.

42. I. The correction officer assuming the duties of a post requiring the supervision of inmates shall examine the entire area of his post for its security and good order only if the correction officer who was just relieved of this post had not reported all secure and in good order within the previous three hours.
    II. A member of the department shall not indulge in any undue familiarity with inmates nor shall he permit any familiarity, on the part of inmates, toward him.

43. When time is NOT a factor, a supervisor enhances both initiative and cooperation by using which one of the following orders?

    A. Command
    B. Plea
    C. Detailed written instructions
    D. Suggestion

44. The development of a *grapevine* or a *rumor clinic* in an institution is USUALLY the result of

    A. the constant provocation of gossip by a few problem individuals
    B. unofficial approval of this employee activity
    C. lack of adequate communication through official channels
    D. employees' disapproval of the administration

45. Appraisal of an employee during his probationary period by an immediate supervisor who happens to be a personal friend of the employee is

    A. *unacceptable* because familiarity results in favoritism
    B. *unacceptable* because people on probation should not be evaluated by immediate supervisors
    C. *acceptable* because it encourages other employees to perform their duties in a manner satisfactory to the appraiser
    D. *acceptable* because the familiarity of the appraiser helps in a complete evaluation

46. In planning the weekly work routine, it is MOST important for a supervisor to

    A. ask employees which assignments they would prefer
    B. ask for volunteers to perform routine tasks
    C. indicate the daily anticipated attendance
    D. list areas of priority interest

47. Of the following, which is NOT a recommended practice of a supervisor?

    A. Giving reasons for emergency assignments or overtime work
    B. Attempting to detect a deep neurosis by examination of work habits or observation of behavior
    C. Taking corrective disciplinary action when an employee fails to improve his attendance following a corrective interview
    D. Consulting with employees as to the best way of getting a job done

48. If a correction officer attended a preparatory class on supervisory techniques, he would MOST likely be instructed that a good supervisor is one who

    A. believes in strong and centralized administrative control
    B. is extremely ambitious
    C. maintains a favorable attitude towards those he encounters
    D. maintains his own method of handling problems

49. Of the following, the MOST important consideration for recommending a provisional promotion to captain should be the correction officer's

    A. capacity to take disciplinary action
    B. ability to control inmate movement
    C. detailed knowledge of departmental rules and regulations
    D. seniority

50. The parts of the decision-making process are GENERALLY the
    I. research of background material
    II. development of details of alternative plans of action
    III. study and interpretation of collected data
    IV. selection of the best course of action
    V. statement of purpose or need

    The CORRECT answer is:

    A. I, II
    B. I, III, V
    C. I, III, IV, V
    D. All of the above

KEY (CORRECT ANSWERS)

1. D	11. D	21. B	31. B	41. A
2. B	12. A	22. D	32. D	42. C
3. A	13. D	23. A	33. B	43. D
4. C	14. C	24. A	34. C	44. C
5. B	15. C	25. C	35. B	45. A
6. D	16. B	26. A	36. A	46. D
7. B	17. A	27. D	37. D	47. B
8. C	18. C	28. B	38. C	48. C
9. B	19. A	29. D	39. C	49. A
10. C	20. D	30. A	40. D	50. D

TEST 2

DIRECTIONS: Each question or incomplete statement is followed by several suggested answers or completions. Select the one that BEST answers the question or completes the statement. *PRINT THE LETTER OF THE CORRECT ANSWER IN THE SPACE AT THE RIGHT.*

1. A threat to institutional order arises from the behavior of the *resister,* the inmate who flagrantly refuses to cooperate with staff. One study has shown that the *resister* exhibits certain characteristics.
   A characteristic NOT exhibited by *resisters* is

   A. a lower average intelligence than other prisoners
   B. a greater tendency toward sadism
   C. poorer preprison employment records
   D. fewer contacts with families while in prison

   1.____

2. Which of the following is NOT a correct reason for the persistence of the inmate social system?

   A. Conformity with inmate values, beliefs, and behavior provides prestige for the inmate.
   B. Inmates frequently complain of being forced to live with other inmates who are inferior and vicious; consequently, they seek acceptance by like inmates as a way of protection against the physical aggression of inferior inmates.
   C. Confinement threatens the masculinity of the inmate; inmates are motivated to overreact to confinement and loss of the masculine self-image by open support of the masculine values of aggressiveness.
   D. At least one-third of all inmates possess the inborn, hostile instincts of primitive humanity and, since this is a high percentage, inmate social systems tend to reflect the patterns of behavior of this aggressive population.

   2.____

3. According to recognized authorities, the population in a prison is together sufficiently large to create regularities in behavior.
   This means that

   A. the regularities require a de-emphasis of coercion and an emphasis on counseling and psychiatric therapy
   B. confinement is an experience requiring major continuous readjustments
   C. the regularities reflect the efforts of employees and inmates to achieve goals and meet problems
   D. the regularities in a prison imply the systematic lack of concern for the dignity of the individual

   3.____

4. The concept of occupation is useful for differentiating criminal behavior systems according to the degree of commitment to criminal values and to the degree to which it qualifies as a career.
   This statement implies that

   A. a person is less intensively committed to criminality when his feelings about himself and his behavior reflect the criminal group's attitudes toward him
   B. when an individual is strongly committed to a criminal culture, the consistency of his crime-oriented behavior is difficult to redirect through rehabilitative programs

   4.____

C. to *go straight* would cause the inmate to appear *honest* in the sense that his previous personal adjustment to daily recurring events would no longer appear consistent
D. professional career criminals regard violence and use of weapons as a mark of resourcefulness not possessed by ordinary career criminals

5. The statement below which most contemporary criminologists would find MOST accurate is that

   A. criminal behavior is explained by the lack of freedom in a materialistic society
   B. although criminal behavior is learned, it is not learned like most social behavior
   C. the process of becoming a criminal is regarded as the same as all personality development
   D. although criminal techniques are learned, the basic origin of criminality lies in inborn defects

6. Central to the association between urbanization and deviant behavior in American society is the problem neighborhood. Such neighborhoods are generally characterized by all of the following factors EXCEPT

   A. great cultural diversity
   B. total community disorganization
   C. general social instability
   D. high population turnover

7. An authority states that, although urbanization and industrialization have tended to standardize behavior, they have also increased the possibility of deviant behavior.
   This means MOST NEARLY that

   A. crime statistics tend to underestimate crimes in rural areas
   B. population density in industrialized cities favors the criminal because sheer numbers, coupled with the close personal relationship characteristic of city life, provides a great many customers for organized crime per 1,000 population
   C. urbanized areas have higher rates for all major crimes because city police systems are understaffed and lack public support
   D. the city-dweller is forced into mechanical conformity but has also been released from traditional constraints

8. Based on authority, the MOST accurate statement concerning the relationship between intelligence and criminality is that

   A. general intelligence as measured by I.Q. tests is unaffected by the individual's cultural background
   B. mental deficiency, by itself, can result in crime
   C. persons at the highest mental levels do not become criminals
   D. mental deficiency may reduce criminality by insulating the individual from frustrations

9. The basic distinction between the professional and non-professional criminal is that the professional criminal

   A. breaks the law more often than the nonprofessional
   B. sees himself as a criminal with a definite means of livelihood, whereas the nonprofessional still retains the basic morals of the dominant society
   C. is part of the larger society, whereas the nonprofessional is isolated from the dominant society
   D. has pride in his criminal techniques, but feels a sense of compassion for his victims, whereas the nonprofessional has neither pride in his techniques nor does he have any sense of guilt

10. Based on objective discussion of the general theory of *white-collar crime*, this type of crime can BEST be defined as any crime committed by a person of respectability and high social _____.

    A. status in the course of his occupation
    B. status in the course of his occupation, excluding crimes of the medical and legal professions, which are generally handled by administrative rather than judicial agencies
    C. status in the course of his occupation, excluding crimes not part of his occupational procedures
    D. status

11. The THREE major ideologies, or systems of belief, affecting law enforcement, court, and correctional activities are the punitive, therapeutic, and preventive ideologies.
    Of the following, the MOST correct statement is that the

    A. therapeutic ideology rather than the punitive or preventive ideology is recognized as offering the ultimate promise for reducing crime
    B. preventive ideology seeks to promote healthy personality development by means of immediate and drastic social changes so that criminals will engage in socially approved conduct
    C. therapeutic ideology considers the criminal to be a victim of defective conditioning of his personality and, consequently, generally seeks a lifetime clinical treatment approach by specially trained psychiatrists
    D. punitive ideology affords the most immediate relief for the requirements of the offended society

12. Group therapy commonly used in the treatment of offenders is intended to have each of the following benefits EXCEPT

    A. creation of a model inmate not demonstrating any potentiality for behavioral change
    B. encouragement of members of the group to see meanings they previously failed to recognize
    C. modification of staff and inmate cultures which are barriers to rehabilitation programs
    D. changing of attitudes in such areas as discipline and authority relationships

13. Crime rates vary with the age of the offender. American data show that the age range which has the highest ARREST RATE is

    A. ages 36 to 45
    B. ages 26 to 35
    C. ages 15 to 25
    D. a figure which cannot be estimated because of the great variations in different kinds of crimes committed by different age groups

14. Prisoners differ in their escape-proneness.
    The following sets of factors are generally associated with the escape behavior of prison inmates EXCEPT set

    A. mental stability and superior intelligence
       cooperative attitude
       mature when first arrested
    B. poor employment record
       uncooperative attitude
       daring and aggressive personality
    C. weak home ties
       habitual offender
       age less than 30 years
    D. poor employment record
       mental instability and inferior intelligence
       served less than 40 percent of his term

15. The correctional agency is an element in the system of criminal justice, which in turn is subject to the social-cultural environment of which it is a product and for which it is a social control instrumentality.
    This statement MOST NEARLY means that

    A. prisons very rarely change
    B. prisons must change if society is to reform
    C. prisons, courts, and police are part of society
    D. the police and courts have a negative impact on prisons

16. Which one of the following statements regarding probation and parole is MOST correct?

    A. Both probation and parole have similarities in objectives, in the use of casework, and in promotion of rehabilitation.
    B. Both probation and parole have similarities in the use of casework and in promotion of rehabilitation, but are dissimilar in their social objectives.
    C. Parole tries to promote change within the offender, whereas probation stresses that punishments should be standardized on the basis of the crime.
    D. Probation generally involves the more serious, criminalistic offender.

17. Walled prisons have been criticized for depriving inmates of normal contact with the outside community and for imposing a daily regime of frustration and aimlessness. The *open institution* has been advocated as an answer to such criticism.
Of the following pairs of statements, the pair which is TRUE is:

   A. I. Penologists generally agree that the open institution will replace the closed prison.
      II. To obtain properly selected inmates, the open institution requires the outside community as the source of its population.
   B. I. Penologists generally agree that the open institution requires the closed prison as the source of its population.
      II. To obtain properly selected inmates, the open institution requires the closed prison as the source of its population.
   C. I. Penologists generally agree that the open institution will replace the closed prison.
      II. Psychological controls are substituted for physical barriers against escape from the open institution.
   D. I. Penologists generally agree that the open institution will not replace the closed prison.
      II. The open institution is far less expensive to construct and to operate than the closed prison.

18. Prison industrial supervisors in this country have generally been accustomed to using excessive numbers of prisoners because

   A. the inmates' qualities as workers usually depress productivity
   B. it is difficult to strike a proper balance between vocational training for prisoner rehabilitation and the achievement of high production for its own sake
   C. prison industrial work is a real asset to vocational training
   D. of the stigma attached to prison-made goods

19. Increases in recidivist rates can result from

   A. more liberal enforcement of parole supervision
   B. increased use of probation by the courts
   C. stricter enforcement of probation supervision
   D. more liberal law enforcement

20. In recent developments in crime prevention, a basic theme has been *reaching the unreached.*
A disproportionate share of the *unreached* consists of

   A. college students arrested for campus demonstrations
   B. multi-problem families
   C. children of affluent suburbia who have been arrested for marijuana possession
   D. highly literate individuals who have been sentenced to correctional institutions for violation of the draft laws

21. Which one of the following statements is correct according to William D. Teeke's article, *Collective Violence in Correctional Institutions,* in a memorable issue of the AMERICAN JOURNAL OF CORRECTION?
    Riots are MORE likely to occur in the

    A. January-June period; the beginning of a new calendar year brings hope for a change in the correctional system in general
    B. January-June period; the densely populated Eastern coastal region is usually in the grip of a cold wave and this, coupled with defective heating systems in old institutions, creates many grievances
    C. July-December period; there is no definite evidence as to why this is the most probable time
    D. July-December period; people are hot and most troubled, and, living in dirty and cramped quarters, under close restraint, seek to rebel

21.____

Questions 22-26.

DIRECTIONS: Questions 22 through 26 consist of passages of one or more sentences. Each of the passages contains an incorrectly used word. First, decide which is the incorrectly used word. Then, from among the options given, decide which word, when substituted for the incorrectly used word, makes the meaning of the passage clear.

SAMPLE QUESTION

Prisoners frequently bring hazards to compel prison officials to allow them more medical care of different medical care than has been provided by the prison physician.
They rarely succeed.
    A. negligence   B. mistreatment
    C. actions   D. evaluations

The word *hazards* in the passage does not convey the meaning the passage is evidently intended to convey. The word *actions* (answer C), when substituted for the word *hazards,* makes the meaning of the passage clear. Accordingly, the answer to the question is C.

22. In the years since passage of the Harrison Narcotic Act of 1914, making the possession of opium amphetamines illegal in most circumstances, drug use has become a subject of considerable scientific interest and investigation.
    There is at present a voluminous literature on drug use of various kinds.

    A. Ingestion   B. Derivatives
    C. Addiction   D. Opiates

22.____

23. Of course, the fact that criminal laws are extremely patterned in definition does not mean that the majority of persons who violate them are dealt with as criminals. Quite the contrary, for a great many forbidden acts are voluntarily engaged in within situations of privacy and go unobserved and unreported.

    A. Symbolic   B. Casual
    C. Scientific   D. Broad-gauged

23.____

24. The most punitive way to study punishment is to focus attention on the pattern of punitive action: to study how a penalty is applied, to study what is done to or taken from an offender.

    A. Characteristic   B. Degrading
    C. Objective   D. Distinguished

24.____

25. The most common forms of punishment in times past have been death, physical torture, mutilation, branding, public humiliation, fines, forfeits of property, banishment, transportation, and imprisonment.
Although this list is by no means differentiated, practically every form of punishment has had several variations and applications.

    A. Specific
    B. Simple
    C. Exhaustive
    D. Characteristic

26. There is another important line of inference between ordinary and professional criminals, and that is the source from which they are recruited.
The professional criminal seems to be drawn from legitimate employment and, in many instances, from parallel vocations or pursuits.

    A. Demarcation
    B. Justification
    C. Superiority
    D. Reference

27. Of the following, what should generally be the MAJOR objective of the institution in dealing with a prisoner?
Focus on

    A. helping him adjust to institutional life
    B. helping him develop his latent talents
    C. helping him prepare for a new career once out of prison
    D. his adjustment to freedom in the community

28. Of the following, the reason which BEST explains why outstanding authorities on penology believe that one city prison may not always be the BEST location for all inmates is that

    A. incarcerating second time offenders in city institutions increases their exposure to the bad influences of their criminal acquaintances
    B. some offenders may have problems which require treatment away from their local environment
    C. incarcerated individuals would be less prone to recidivism in a rural environment
    D. penal institutions on islands have a tendency to increase inmate tensions

29. Under the criminal treatment system, the justification for treating the condition of the individual is the fact that he has engaged in criminal conduct.
In the civil treatment system, the justification for treating the condition is

    A. always related to the crime
    B. given by the courts
    C. never related to the crime
    D. may or may not be related to the crime

30. On the basis of recent trends, which of the following statements would be INCORRECT?

    A. Less than one-quarter of the sentenced prisoners incarcerated in locally operated institutions can be considered civil prisoners.
    B. Many of the persons sentenced to local institutions have either been incarcerated in, or are destined to be incarcerated in, institutions administered by the state.
    C. Most of the persons incarcerated under sentence throughout the state today are first offenders.
    D. There is no reliable evidence to show that education or vocational training applied on a general basis has any effect in reducing recidivism.

31. There are two basic rationales for subjecting persons to treatment: one is called the *civil* system; and the other is called the *criminal* system.
Of the following, the BASIC difference between these two systems is

    A. that the civil system is used to administer justice to those first time offenders who have committed a mild crime
    B. that the civil system usually requires facilities or institutions separate from those of the criminal system
    C. the criminal institution's employment of more highly skilled personnel
    D. the degree of exposure to community life

32. The MAJOR purpose of the recreational facilities located atop a major house of detention for men is to

    A. allow inmates a greater opportunity to socialize and expose themselves to sunshine
    B. enable fewer guards to watch inmates so the cost of institutional operations can be decreased
    C. allow greater freedom of movement of inmates within the confines of the institution
    D. provide relaxing and exhausting activities which will remove tension

33. A group of 50 youths is currently commuting from a local prison to an experimental training program in group counseling.
The purpose of this program is

    A. basically to enable the inmates to serve as counselors for their fellow inmates
    B. chiefly to stimulate inmates and prepare them for future college training
    C. to expose inmates who have almost completed their sentence to civilian community life
    D. chiefly to prepare them for employment at the completion of their incarceration

34. A recent ruling by the courts held that no citizen awaiting trial be held in detention for more than _____ days.

    A. 90   B. 60   C. 30   D. 120

Questions 35-39.

DIRECTIONS: Questions 35 through 39 are based on the following tables.

Forest City, an imaginary jurisdiction, classifies its offenders as juvenile delinquents, youthful offenders, or adult offenders. There are two institutions for female offenders and five institutions for male offenders. Table A shows the average daily number of inmates for the years shown. Table B shows what percentage of average daily number of male inmates for the years shown were juvenile delinquents, youthful offenders, or adult offenders.

TABLE A - FOREST CITY INMATES

Institutions for Female Offenders:	1990	2000	2001 (estimate)
(1) Pleasantdale	70	105	120
(2) Shady Valley	W	190	210
TOTAL	195	295	330
Institutions for Male Offenders:			
(1) Leadurney	260	320	310
(2) Sherman	110	130	Y
(3) Riveredge	1700	1800	1850
(4) Thompson	650	800	Z
(5) Maxim	1200	1625	1700
TOTAL	3920	4675	5030
TOTAL MALE & FEMALE	X	4970	5360

TABLE B - FOREST CITY OFFENDERS
PERCENTAGE OF AVERAGE DAILY NUMBER OF INMATES CLASSIFIED AS JUVENILE DELINQUENTS, YOUTHFUL OFFENDERS, OR ADULT OFFENDERS
(See Code Below)

	1990			2000		
	A	B	C	A	B	C
Institutions for Female Offenders:						
(1) Pleasantdale	20%	60%	20%	25%	75%	-
(2) Shady Valley	15%	30%	55%	-	35%	65%
Institutions for Male Offenders:						
(1) Leadurney	5%	95%	-	80%	20%	-
(2) Sherman	10%	35%	55%	10%	35%	55%
(3) Riveredge	90%	10%	-	85%	15%	-
(4) Thompson	-	40%	60%	-	35%	65%
(5) Maxim	-	20%	80%	-	5%	95%

CODE
A - JUVENILE OFFENDERS
B - YOUTHFUL OFFENDERS
C - ADULT OFFENDERS

35. From 1990 to 2000, the average daily number of female youthful offenders in the Pleasantdale institution increased MOST NEARLY by

    A. 20
    B. 29
    C. 37
    D. a figure greater than 40

36. One of the following sets of figures belongs in the circled spaces marked Y and Z. Which one of the following sets of figures LOGICALLY belongs in these spaces?

    A. 115 and 990
    B. 115 and 1050
    C. 120 and 990
    D. 120 and 1050

37. The figures which LOGICALLY belong in the circled spaces marked W and X are

    A. 125 and 4115
    B. 125 and 4215
    C. 175 and 4115
    D. 175 and 4215

38. In 2000, of the average daily number of Forest City male and female inmates, the percentage to be found in Maxim was MOST NEARLY

    A. 27%   B. 30%   C. 33%   D. 36%

39. In 1990, the average daily number of adult male offenders was MOST NEARLY 39._____

   A. 60 in Sherman and 390 in Thompson
   B. 110 in Sherman and 650 in Thompson
   C. 390 in Thompson and 1300 in Maxim
   D. 800 in Thompson and 1625 in Maxim

Questions 40-43.

DIRECTIONS: Questions 40 through 43 are based on the following passage.

Female criminality is very much under-reported, especially if one considers offenses such as shoplifting, thefts by prostitutes, offenses against children, and homicide. There are even certain offenses such as homosexuality and exhibitionism that go practically unprosecuted if committed by women. Female offenders are really protected by men, even by victims, who are usually disinclined to complain to authorities. Since women play much less active roles in society than men do, one must be prepared for the fact that women are often the instigators of crimes committed by men and, as instigators, they are hard to detect. There are several crimes that are ordinarily highly detectable in men but have very low detectability in women. Her roles as homemaker, mother, nurse, wife, and so forth, permit the female to commit a crime and yet screen that crime from public view—for example, slowly poisoning her husband or treating her children abusively. In addition, law enforcement officers, judges, and juries are much more lenient toward women than toward men. Such considerations lead to the conclusion that criminality of women is largely masked criminality. Consequently, official statistics and records of criminality should be expected to under-report female offenses. The true measure of female crime must be sought from unofficial sources. The masked character of female crime and its gross under-reporting are consistent with the official view that the female is a very low risk for crime.

40. What has the writer inferred about the incidence of female offenses? 40._____

   A. It gives an adequate representation of the number of crimes committed by men but instigated by women.
   B. It is not to be considered an important area of criminality.
   C. It is understated because the classic female role makes her less visible to social scrutiny.
   D. In every crime the incidence of male offenses is more difficult to detect than that of women.

41. Judges are inclined to be lenient toward female offenders because 41._____

   A. the role of the woman in society has stereotyped her as maternal and non-hostile
   B. the majority of their crimes do not physically harm others
   C. they commit crimes which are difficult to detect
   D. official statistics report them as less likely to commit crimes

42. Of the following, the title MOST suitable for this passage is 42._____

   A. Male Criminality
   B. The Petty Offender
   C. The Female Murderer
   D. Exposing Female Criminality

43. According to the passage, which of the following crimes is LEAST likely to be prosecuted against a woman?

    A. Child abuse
    B. Exhibitionism
    C. Homicide
    D. Prostitution

Questions 44-47.

DIRECTIONS: Questions 44 through 47 are based on the following passage.

The usual explanation for drunken behavior is that alcohol, which is a physiological depressant impairs reasoning and inhibition powers before it depresses the ability to act and to express emotion.

The purely physiological effects of alcohol are very much like those of fatigue. Individual personality and social and cultural influences apparently greatly determine how these effects are reflected in changed behavior as alcohol is consumed. Therefore, one can assert that alcohol alone does not cause drunken behavior; rather, drunken behavior expresses personal character, cultural traditions, and social circumstances, as they influence a person's reactions to the physiological effects of alcohol on his body.

For some people, and in some circumstances, these personal, cultural, and social factors may readily express themselves as criminal behavior. The most obvious case, of course, is public drunkenness.

The exact relationship between various crimes and various stages of intoxication is not completely known. G.M. Scott believes that the moderate stages of intoxication are the ones usually associated with crime, since the latter states of intoxication make performance of crime impossible. Dr. Banay found that many drunks are drawn into crime not only by the need of money to replace wages that drinking prevents them from earning, but also by their increased irritability and pugnacity.... He discovered that most of the sex offenses for which offenders are committed to state prisons show a relation between alcohol and the crime and that the average sex case is a clear-cut illustration of the hypothesis that alcohol covers up an underlying condition and that some dormant tendency is either brought to the surface or aggravated by alcohol.

In addition to drunken behavior resulting in criminal acts, it is also connected to several other important social problems. Reference can be made particularly to dependency, unemployment, desertion, divorce, vagrancy, and suicide. For all of these social ills, alcohol acts as the physiological depressing agent which influences one's deviation from normative behavior.

44. Discussions of intoxication customarily state that alcohol

    A. initially affects the analytic faculty
    B. initially affects the ability to express feelings
    C. reduces the desire for money
    D. stimulates perception of the true nature of one's condition

45. Which one of the following hypotheses would Dr. Banay MOST likely support?   45._____

    A. The casual drinker is less likely to commit a crime than the chronic drinker.
    B. An aggressive drunk is likely to have aggressive tendencies when not under the influence of alcohol.
    C. The underlying cause of most sex offenses is excessive drinking.
    D. There is no connection between cultural background and drunken behavior.

46. The title BEST suited for this passage is: 46._____

    A. How Alcohol Influences Potential Sexual Offenders
    B. Stages of Intoxication
    C. The Role of Alcoholic Consumption in Human Behavior
    D. The Relationship Between Alcohol and Emotion

47. The writer implies that   47._____

    A. a desire to destroy oneself is a frequent side effect of drinking intoxicating liquors
    B. a person who is drunk may find it easier to kill himself
    C. there is a pattern of drinking behavior in the background of most suicides
    D. there is no relationship between the problems of drinking and suicide

Questions 48-50.

DIRECTIONS: Questions 48 through 50 are based on the following passage.

A survey of the drinking behavior of 1,185 persons representing the adult population of Iowa in 2008 aged 21 years and older revealed that approximately 40 percent were abstainers. Of the nearly 1 million drinkers in the State, 47 percent were classed as light drinkers, 37 percent as moderate, and 16 percent as heavy drinkers. Twenty-two percent of the men drinkers were classed as heavy drinkers but only 8 percent of the women drinkers. The proportion of heavy drinkers increased with level of education among drinkers residing in the city –from 15 percent of the least educated to 22 percent of the most educated but decreased among farm residents from 17 percent of the least educated to 4 percent of the most educated. Age differences in the extent of drinking were not pronounced. The age class of 36-45 had the lowest proportions of light drinkers while the age class 61 and over had the lowest proportion of heavy drinkers.

48. Of the total drinking population in Iowa, how many were moderate drinkers?   48._____

    A. 370,000   B. 438   C. 370   D. 438,150

49. What percent of the men drinkers surveyed were NOT heavy drinkers?   49._____

    A. 60%
    C. 78%
    B. 84%
    D. Cannot be determined

50. According to the passage, which one of the following statements concerning heavy drinking would be CORRECT?   50._____

    A. Experts are in sharp conflict regarding the reason for heavy drinking.
    B. The amount of heavy drinking in the city is directly proportional to the amount of education.
    C. The degree of heavy drinking is directly proportional to the age class of the drinkers.
    D. The degree of heavy drinking is inversely to the number of light drinkers.

KEY (CORRECT ANSWERS)

1. A	11. D	21. C	31. B	41. A
2. D	12. A	22. B	32. D	42. D
3. C	13. C	23. D	33. D	43. B
4. B	14. A	24. C	34. A	44. A
5. C	15. C	25. C	35. C	45. B
6. B	16. A	26. A	36. D	46. C
7. D	17. B	27. D	37. A	47. B
8. D	18. A	28. B	38. C	48. A
9. B	19. C	29. D	39. A	49. C
10. C	20. B	30. C	40. C	50. B

READING COMPREHENSION
UNDERSTANDING AND INTERPRETING WRITTEN MATERIAL
EXAMINATION SECTION
TEST 1

DIRECTIONS: Each question or incomplete statement is followed by several suggested answers or completions. Select the one that BEST answers the question or completes the statement. *PRINT THE LETTER OF THE CORRECT ANSWER IN THE SPACE AT THE RIGHT.*

Questions 1-4.

DIRECTIONS: Questions 1 through 4 are to be answered SOLELY on the basis of the following passage.

Morally, there is no basis for the assertion that the commission of a social offense allows society to strip a human being of all his rights except those which, through some sort of *natural law* concept, he needs to survive. Rather, society is justified in punishing offenders only to the extent that it needs to protect itself; excessive retribution is *immoral.* Thus, unless society can demonstrate that a specific deprivation is necessary to its self-preservation, or to its reassertion of authority over the individual offender, it should not be entitled to enforce the deprivation. To place the burden on the prisoner to demonstrate that he should not be deprived of a particular right appears to be unfair and unjustified for two reasons: (1) the resources and skills are unequally distributed in society's favor, and (2) the concept of *proportionality* as a rudimentary value is rejected by such an approach, which even theories of retribution and vengeance do not support.

Pragmatically, too, prisoners should be viewed and treated as human beings. Ninety-five percent of all those incarcerated in prisons are returned to the free world. It violates common sense to expect a man who has been treated at best as a cipher while in prison to be enamored of a society which has not only enchained him but also has increased his torment while he is confined. When he is released, his action is likely to be antisocial rather than social. Additionally, the imposition of excessive suffering on offenders permeates society's attitudes toward others in its midst. Just as we are now realizing that violence abroad erodes the barriers against domestic violence, official hostility toward some human beings tends to add an aura of authority to hostility toward and among others. Disinclination to cherish humanity at one point in society leads to total abdication of humanity at another.

1. In the above passage, it is pointed out that 1.____

    A. it is a practical approach to treatment to take away all but the basic rights of a prisoner
    B. it is proper to remove an inmate's rights within a system of rewards and punishments
    C. incarceration should not be used for revenge against one who has offended society
    D. the inmate ought to play a primary role in determining treatment methods

2. According to the above passage,

   A. inmates who are treated badly are apt to resort to antisocial behavior when they are returned to society
   B. there is a tendency among inmates to join organizations dedicated to achieving civil rights for the victims of society
   C. society generally sees all inmates as being equal, despite inconsistent observation of prisoners' rights
   D. recidivism is a serious problem for the majority of prisoners who are released on parole

3. While criticizing the kind of treatment prisoners receive in our institutions, the above passage implies that

   A. the mistreatment of prisoners is an outcome of society's benign attitude toward the law-abiding citizen
   B. cruelty begets cruelty, and that humane treatment will make better citizens of those entrusted to our care
   C. when violence in this country spreads, it increases all over the world
   D. an aura of authority has replaced official hostility in correctional institutions

4. According to the above passage, penal authorities are justified in depriving prisoners of rights

   A. in order to satisfy society's desire for retribution against criminal offenders
   B. until prisoners can demonstrate that particular deprivations are unjustified
   C. whenever the preservation of order within the institution will be facilitated
   D. only when it is necessary to protect society or maintain control over the inmate

Questions 5-8.

DIRECTIONS: Questions 5 through 8 are to be answered SOLELY on the basis of the following excerpt from a memo circulated by a correction official for comments.

Some bargaining is virtually inevitable between those charged with enforcing institutional regulations and inmates who are supposed to be regulated for the simple reason that administrators rarely have sufficient resources to gain complete conformity to all the rules. An insufficient number of guards and cells and inadequately threatening punishments create an environment in which institutional rules are often ignored. At the same time, the attempt to impose order upon individuals deprived of normal amenities, who often lack opportunities for adequate recreation or privacy, tends to produce violent disorder. Toleration by correctional administrators and officers of constant violation of institutional rules results even if confined to a level considered by administrators to be neither very visible nor very serious. Recurring contact between guards and inmates creates ample opportunity for an ongoing informal bargaining.

Although some form of bargaining has long been recognized as a basic process of control within prisons and other total institutions, it is not clear whether a system of control which relies on private, particularized bargains between staff and inmates contributes to the goals of rehabilitation, order, or protection from arbitrary punishment. In fact, within the daily bargaining process, often the only goal sought to be achieved by the institution is short term surface order - the semblance that everything is running smoothly with no official (or public) cause for alarm.

5. According to the above passage, all of the following conditions contribute to the existence of bargaining EXCEPT

   A. difficulty in getting inmates to conform to the rules
   B. the scarcity of guards and cells
   C. the scarcity of administrators
   D. the pressures of confinement brought on by prison conditions

6. According to the above passage, which one of the following is MOST likely to create a climate for bargaining between inmates and staff?

   A. Lack of privacy
   B. Lack of opportunities for recreation
   C. Frequent interaction between guards and inmates
   D. Desires of guards to avoid enforcement of rules

7. The author IMPLIES that the practice of bargaining in institutions is a process which

   A. is not generally recognized outside institutions
   B. eliminates violent disorders among inmates
   C. should be utilized more frequently
   D. has been in existence for a long time

8. According to the above passage, which one of the following statements concerning bargaining is MOST NEARLY correct?
   It

   A. contributes to the goals of the institution because it protects inmates from arbitrary punishment
   B. impedes rehabilitation since it weakens respect for correctional personnel
   C. is a method of reducing the visibility of inmate rule violations
   D. detracts from the smooth operation of the institution because it is an ineffective system of control

Questions 9-12.

DIRECTIONS: Questions 9 through 12 are to be answered on the basis of the following portion of a report submitted by a Tour Commander to the appropriate superior about an unusual occurrence in a Detention Dormitory. The portion of the report consists of 21 numbered sentences, some of which may or may not follow the principles of good report writing.

1. Following is a report of an altercation between inmate John Doe, #441-77-9375, and inmate Henry Green, #441-77-1656.
2. At approximately 6:15 A.M. on June 15, an alarm was received in the Control Room from Officer Arthur Kinney #6214 of the 7M dormitory (General Population).
3. Captain Ronald Doaks #529 and Officer Henry James #7654 responded immediately to determine the cause of the alarm.
4. Captain Doaks reports that, upon arrival, he observed inmate John Doe, #441-77-9375, on the officer's bridge bleeding from the mouth.

5. The institutional doctor also found a stab wound in the left arm.
6. The Captain observed inmate Henry Green, #441-77-1656, locked behind the *B* gate, heard him shouting obscenities and threatening further harm to Officer Kinney.
7. He noticed a large group of inmates standing quietly in the day room.
8. Officer Kinney, who was on post alone, reports he heard a commotion in the rear of the dormitory while sitting at his desk reading the Departmental Rules and Regulations.
9. He could not see what was going on because of a large crowd of inmates.
10. He reports that inmate Doe suddenly broke through the crowd screaming toward the *B* gate.
11. Doe was being pursued by inmate Green.
12. Officer Kinney states that he sounded the alarm and allowed inmate Doe onto the bridge.
13. Since inmate Doe was bleeding from the mouth, Captain Doaks ordered Officer James to escort him to the clinic for immediate examination and treatment by Dr. James White, who subsequently suspected a broken jaw and also discovered a puncture wound in the left bicep.
14. Dr. White ordered his transfer to Harmony Hospital for x-ray of the jaw.
15. Inmate Green, who appeared free of injury, stated to the Captain that he and Doe argued over the telephone, agreed to *take it to the back* and fight.
16. Green would make no further statements.
17. No other inmate in the dormitory would admit seeing anything.
18. Inmate Green received an infraction and was transferred to the Administrative Area pending further investigation.
19. The housing area was then restored to order and normal operations were resumed.
20. Prior to his transfer to the hospital, inmate Doe stated to the Captain that he was assaulted by inmate Green for no apparent reason.
21. He was told that he has an infraction and, upon return from the hospital, would be transferred to another housing unit pending investigation.

9. Of the following, which sentence is MOST likely to be out of sequence?

   A. 2   B. 5   C. 8   D. 14

10. Of the following, which sentence indicates the GREATEST need for further clarification by the Tour Commander submitting the report?

    A. 4   B. 6   C. 9   D. 17

11. Which one of the following sentences BEST indicates the possibility of potential danger remaining in 7M because of the omission of a necessary procedure?

    A. 3   B. 14   C. 19   D. 21

12. Which one of the following sentences is LEAST significant to the report?

    A. 4   B. 7   C. 11   D. 17

Questions 13-16.

DIRECTIONS: Questions 13 through 16 are to be answered SOLELY on the basis of the following fictitious directive which may or may not conform with actual policy and procedure of the Department of Correction.

<u>DIRECTIVE NO. 15</u>   Dated March 1

Guidelines for Members of the Department when accepting packages for inmates being held in custody of the City Department of Correction.

1. <u>Receipt and Distribution of Packages</u>

All packages delivered by the postal authorities must bear the name and address of the sender. All packages regardless of whether received through the mail or delivered by an individual, during visiting hours only, must be in a cardboard box with tape sealing same so as to prevent access to contents of package. When package is received by mail, it is to be placed in the mailroom of the institution concerned by the staff member assigned to picking up the mail. In addition, the officer delivering the package to mailroom officer will get a receipt for all packages. The mailroom officer shall prepare Form P-103 in duplicate, which will document the time and description of all packages received, including the contents thereof, as well as the name and address of the sender. Packages must be weighed and weight noted on Form P-103, as no inmate is to receive an excess of 40 lbs. in packages in a six-month period. Log is to be maintained of all packages received, distributed, and returned to sender, including the weights for packages received and accepted. When a package is brought to the institution by an individual, during visiting hours only, it is to bear the name and address of person who is responsible for articles in package, who must be the individual who is delivering the package. Form P-103 is to remain with package until signed by inmate, since original of Form P-103 is the institutional record and substantiation that inmate has received his/her package.

As soon as practicable, all packages are to be searched for contraband and appropriate actions taken. If package is determined to be acceptable, inmate concerned shall be called to mailroom and shall inspect package, sign Form P-103 in duplicate, receive the duplicate copy of Form P-103, and remove package to his/her respective cell. If the inmate is not available when called for, package is to be secured in a locked closet or room and key so secured that only authorized personnel have access to area. If mailroom officer is not on duty when package is brought to institution by an individual, officer assigned to visits is to be responsible for handling and safekeeping of package according to this directive.

2. <u>Acceptability of Articles</u>

Suitable clothing may be accepted in all packages according to guidelines determined by the head of each institution. However, the institutional clothing card must be referred to so excess clothing is not accumulated and in order to maintain a strict control over same. Food and snacks are also acceptable items - no alcoholic beverages, nor glass containers are to be accepted. Sharp instruments are not to be accepted nor any item that may create a hazard or breach of security within the institution. Shaving utensils are to be distributed by the institution and are not to be accepted in packages. Under no circumstances is money or jewelry to be accepted in packages. No medications are to be accepted when included in packages or otherwise, but, when the occasion arises, inmate must be instructed that all medications are dispensed through the medical staff assigned to that institution. Prescription eyeglasses can be accepted, but must be inspected and approved by the institutional physician before distribution to inmate. Under no circumstances are cigarettes to be accepted in packages since they must be purchased through each institutional commissary.

3. <u>Appropriate Areas For Use</u>

Food received in packages cannot be removed from the housing area. Under no circumstances should an inmate bring food to the main dining room as a substitution or addition to the departmental menu. Books and magazines cannot be removed from the housing areas. Under no condition should any inmate's library privileges be cancelled or modified because he has received publications from another source. All eatable items are to be consumed either in the inmate's cell or the day room of the housing area he/she is assigned to. Any inmate who has received special permission to receive an item of clothing for sporting or athletic purposes may use said clothing only in the gymnasium of the institution, said clothing is to remain in the gymnasium, and a system for laundering determined and controlled by the Recreation Director.

4. A. <u>Safeguarding Undelivered Packages</u>

All undelivered packages will be secured in a locked closet of the mailroom or the mailroom itself. The mailroom shall be secured whenever a custodial member is not in attendance. The key to the mailroom must be secured so that only authorized personnel have access to the area. The schedule for the use of the mailroom must be arranged to create accountability for the safekeeping of all packages received for any inmate of the Department. Every effort must be made to deliver packages to inmates as soon as is practicable. However, if after ten days, the package is not delivered, it must be returned to the sender with an appropriate notation - under no condition may a package remain undelivered for more than ten days.

B. <u>Ensuring that Unacceptable Packages or Unacceptable Items Are Returned to Sender</u>

All unacceptable packages or unacceptable items must be returned to sender immediately upon being determined unacceptable. The inmate must be notified of any article or package that is being returned, but not necessarily before the items have been mailed. Upon mailing any unacceptable items to the sender, no items shall be returned which would violate postal regulations. Whenever articles are returned to sender, a return receipt must be requested of the postal authorities.

5. <u>Procedure for the Prosecution of Persons Violating the Postal Regulations or Prison Contraband Law</u>

Whenever serious contraband is found in a package received by mail at an institution of the Department, the supervisor investigating the incident will notify the postal authorities, cooperating with them whenever possible. The officer who actually finds contraband must be witness to any criminal proceedings that would follow. If contraband is delivered to the institution by an individual, the Police Department shall be notified, and the supervisor investigating said incident will cooperate fully with the Police Department. The officer who actually finds contraband will be a witness if any criminal proceeding is instituted. All serious contraband will be turned over to the Police Department and a voucher received for same. The supervisor will conduct a complete investigation of all discoveries of serious contraband received in packages, and submit proper reports to the head of the institution.

6. <u>System of Appeals for Those Inmates Denied Packages or Contents Thereof</u>

Any inmate who has been denied a package or any article included in a package and has been informed of this by the mailroom officer may request Form P-111, fill out same, and return it to the mailroom officer. This is a form of appeal and must be forwarded to the A/D/W-A/D/S in charge of security, who will investigate the complaint and render a decision on the complaint. The inmate must be interviewed by the A/D/W or A/D/S or a designated person, who will inform him/her of the reason for the denial, and the security Deputy's decision. If the inmate tells the security Deputy he/she wishes to appeal, a copy of the decision and Form P-111 will be forwarded to the D/S or D/W for a final decision. If no appeal is requested after the interview and rendering of the A/D/W-A/D/S - decision, or at the conclusion or final decision by the D/W - D/S, Form P-111 and the written copy of the decision will be filed in the inmate's folder.

7. <u>Procedure for Receiving Special Permission for Items or Articles Not Generally Allowed the Institutional Population, Before the Package is Received</u>

An inmate wishing to receive a specific item who has a legitimate need, may write to the head of the institution stating the need, if the item is not generally allowed in the institution. When determined necessary by the head of the institution, the inmate will be asked to submit a professional opinion substantiating the need. The request and substantiation will be submitted to a review board and their determination will be forwarded to the head of the institution for his/her approval. Only upon receipt of the approval of the head of the institution will special permission be given for possession of a specific item or article.

13. According to the above directive, which one of the following is NOT a condition for receiving a package in an institution of the Department?   13.____

    A. All packages must be weighed and logged in an effort to control the aggregate weight of packages received by each inmate at an institution.
    B. Packages may be brought to the institution by individuals during visiting hours only.
    C. If a package has been determined acceptable by a custodial officer, the inmate shall inspect the package, sign for it, and take possession of it.
    D. The log maintained by the mailroom officer is the institutional substantiation that the inmate has received the package.

14. According to the above directive, which one of the following is NOT a valid statement regarding acceptability of items in packages received for inmates in institutions of the Department?   14.____

    A. Money, jewelry, and medications are not to be accepted in packages.
    B. Prescription eyeglasses can be accepted by the institution before they are approved and inspected by the institutional physician.
    C. Shaving utensils which meet the guidelines established by the head of the institution may be acceptable when received in packages.
    D. The institutional clothing card must be consulted when determining whether to accept clothing in packages.

15. According to the above directive, which one of the following statements is NOT valid concerning actions to be taken when postal regulations or prison contraband laws are violated while sending or delivering packages to an institution?

    A. The officer who discovers serious contraband in a package, whether delivered to an institution by an individual or mailed through the postal authorities, is a witness as far as the Department is concerned.
    B. The supervisor responsible for investigating the discovery of serious contraband in a package brought to the institution by a visitor must notify the Director of Operations immediately.
    C. All serious contraband must be turned over to the Police Department and vouchered, whether or not criminal proceedings are instituted.
    D. The supervisor responsible for investigating the discovery of serious contraband in a package brought to the institution must submit his/her report to the head of the institution.

16. According to the above directive, which one of the following is a VALID statement concerning an application for special permission to receive an article not generally allowed in an institution?

    A. A professional opinion substantiating the need for the item requested must accompany the application for special permission to receive said item.
    B. A review board, upon receipt of the application and professional opinion substantiating the need for the item, will render a final decision.
    C. An inmate wishing to receive a special item, for any reason, may write to the head of the institution.
    D. The head of the institution may approve, for use by a specific inmate, a specific item or article which is not generally permitted in the institution.

Questions 17-19.

DIRECTIONS: Questions 17 through 19 are to be answered SOLELY on the basis of the following passage.

In collaboration with operating staff and research social scientists, the statistician should be responsible for installing standard measures of achievement in the information system. Reliability of measurements used by the system should be reviewed periodically. This review will be especially important if predictive devices are installed to facilitate comparison of expectations with observed outcomes.

This evaluation technique is well suited to standardized use by information systems. A standard base expectancy table is established to predict results of programs for groups, using criteria such as recidivism or completion of training. Such a device will be capable of assigning any given subject to a class of like subjects grouped by the statistical weighting of aggregated characteristics. Group expectancy for success or failure as determined by recidivism or other criteria can be expressed in percentiles.

Use of base expectancies for comparison with observed outcomes may be thought of as a *soft* method of evaluation. But its economy, in comparison with the classical control group procedure, is considerable. It eliminates the need for routine management of research controls over extended periods. Comparison of predicted with observed outcome affords a rough estimate of program effectiveness. For example, if the average expected recidivism of a group of offenders exposed to a behavior modification program is 50 percent, but the observed outcome is 25 percent, a *prima facie* indication of program effectiveness is established.

Such an indication affords the administrator some assurance that a program seriously subjected to a controlled evaluation with similar results is continuing to be effective. It may also provide a rough estimate of the value of a program that has not been evaluated under the control group method. This kind of evaluation has many limitations. A predictive device is valid only to the extent that the group observed is typical of the population used as the basis for the standard. A second objection to the use of predictive devices in evaluation rests on the tendency of the predictive bases to deteriorate. The applicability of a prediction under circumstances prevailing in year one will not necessarily be the same circumstance prevailing in year ten. Accordingly, it is good practice to audit the accuracy of the predictive device at least every five years to assure that the circumstances are the same. A final objection is that predictive devices can be used only for global indications of program effectiveness.

17. Of the following, the KEY element in the traditional approach to program evaluation that would NOT be used in the approach described in the passage is

    A. computers
    B. recidivism rates
    C. standard populations
    D. control groups

17.____

18. Of the following, the MOST appropriate title for the above passage is

    A. HOW TO PREDICT THE RESULTS OF PROGRAM EVALUATIONS
    B. A *SOFT* METHOD OF PROGRAM EVALUATION
    C. THE USE OF PREDICTIVE DEVICES IN PROGRAM EVALUATION
    D. COOPERATION BETWEEN THE STATISTICIAN AND OPERATING STAFF

18.____

19. All of the following statements describe limitations of using predictive devices to evaluate programs for the first time EXCEPT:

    A. The group under study must be typical of the group used to develop the predictive device.
    B. Predictive devices can be used only for global indications of program effectiveness.
    C. Predictive devices are more expensive to use than classical control group procedure.
    D. The circumstances prevailing in the year of the study must be the same as in the year the predictive device was developed.

19.____

Questions 20-25.

DIRECTIONS: Questions 20 through 25 are to be answered SOLELY on the basis of the following passage.

At present, in State X, whole classes of offenders are retained at unnecessarily close and expensive levels of confinement and supervision because the various decision-makers involved are required to make predictions about the future behavior of offenders which cannot, given the present state of social science, be made accurately. Items such as social and psychological history, changes in attitude, estimates of institutional progress, and anticipation of constructive responses to parole supervision are particularly useless as evaluative criteria in the disposition of offenders because such subjective evaluations are rooted in the attitudes of the appraiser and in the constructive tendencies of bureaucracies.

The result has been that while probation is used extensively (chiefly because institutions are overcrowded) parole board policy has become increasingly cautious and expensive. Although the initial choice between probation and commitment to prison is often arbitrary, the offender thus committed tends to remain incarcerated for long periods. Because the absence of a clear, positive, and legislatively authorized parole policy is a fundamental obstacle to the reallocation of funds, and because the decision problems involved are repeated at each level of the correctional system, the Committee on Criminal Penalties examined the state parole policy. It then presented model legislation which required that offenders committed to prison be automatically released to parole at expiration of the statutory minimum parole-eligible period (often only six months under present law), unless their individual histories contained substantial evidence of past serious violence. The resulting institutional savings were to be devoted chiefly to improving parole services and subsidies for improvements in local law enforcement agencies.

The basic intent of the legislation was to substitute clearly defined statutory ineligibility for release criteria based on the past actions of offenders for the present administratively defined eligibility criteria that necessarily rely on predictive data of highly questionable validity. By requiring the early release of any offender not shown to be clearly ineligible, the act would essentially remove responsibility for the disposition of doubtful cases from the parole authorities and return it to the courts.

20. Of the following, the MOST suitable title for the above passage is

   A. THE REASONS FOR GRANTING PAROLE
   B. THE COMMITTEE ON CRIMINAL PENALTIES
   C. DECISION PROBLEMS IN CORRECTIONS
   D. A NEW APPROACH IN PAROLE POLICY

21. According to the above passage, which of the following is NOT a true statement about the present correctional system in State X?

   A. Many offenders are retained at unnecessarily close and expensive levels of confinement and supervision.
   B. The offenders committed to prison tend to remain incarcerated for long periods.
   C. Probation has become more and more extensive in application chiefly because institutions are overcrowded.
   D. When reviewing cases, parole authorities often use objective criteria like the social and psychological history of inmates.

22. According to the above passage, one change from the present system of parole which would result from the enactment of the proposed system of parole is that

   A. criminals could be paroled after the minimum parole eligibility period
   B. offenders who committed serious violent acts would automatically be paroled after a specified amount of time
   C. institutions would become overcrowded
   D. responsibility for parole in doubtful cases would essentially be given to the court rather than the parole authorities

23. According to the proposed method of determining parole, an inmate would be paroled after a specified period

   A. unless ineligible by administrative criteria
   B. unless ineligible by specific legislative criteria
   C. if eligible according to administrative criteria
   D. if eligible according to specific legislative criteria

23._____

24. Under the proposed method of determining parole, parole would be granted or denied depending on the inmate's

   A. past actions
   B. present behavior
   C. present psychological adjustment
   D. probable future actions

24._____

25. According to the above passage, the one of the following that is NOT a primary reason why the Committee on Criminal Penalties presented the legislation described above was to

   A. set objective criteria for parole
   B. expedite the reallocation of funds
   C. eliminate arbitrary commitment to prison
   D. prevent overlong commitment of many inmates

25._____

KEY (CORRECT ANSWERS)

1.	C	11.	C
2.	A	12.	B
3.	B	13.	D
4.	D	14.	C
5.	C	15.	B
6.	C	16.	D
7.	D	17.	D
8.	C	18.	C
9.	B	19.	C
10.	B	20.	D

21.	D
22.	D
23.	B
24.	A
25.	C

PREPARING WRITTEN MATERIAL

PARAGRAPH REARRANGEMENT
COMMENTARY

The sentences that follow are in scrambled order. You are to rearrange them in proper order and indicate the letter choice containing the correct answer at the space at the right.

Each group of sentences in this section is actually a paragraph presented in scrambled order. Each sentence in the group has a place in that paragraph; no sentence is to be left out. You are to read each group of sentences and decide upon the best order in which to put the sentences so as to form a well-organized paragraph.

The questions in this section measure the ability to solve a problem when all the facts relevant to its solution are not given.

More specifically, certain positions of responsibility and authority require the employee to discover connection between events sometimes, apparently, unrelated. In order to do this, the employee will find it necessary to correctly infer that unspecified events have probably occurred or are likely to occur. This ability becomes especially important when action must be taken on incomplete information.

Accordingly, these questions require competitors to choose among several suggested alternatives, each of which presents a different sequential arrangement of the events. Competitors must choose the MOST logical of the suggested sequences.

In order to do so, they may be required to draw on general knowledge to infer missing concepts or events that are essential to sequencing the given events. Competitors should be careful to infer only what is essential to the sequence. The plausibility of the wrong alternatives will always require the inclusion of unlikely events or of additional chains of events which are NOT essential to sequencing the given events.

It's very important to remember that you are looking for the best of the four possible choices, and that the best choice of all may not even be one of the answers you're given to choose from.

There is no one right way to solve these problems. Many people have found it helpful to first write out the order of the sentences, as they would have arranged them, on their scrap paper before looking at the possible answers. If their optimum answer is there, this can save them some time. If it isn't, this method can still give insight into solving the problem. Others find it most helpful to just go through each of the possible choices, contrasting each as they go along. You should use whatever method feels comfortable and works for you.

While most of these types of questions are not that difficult, we've added a higher percentage of the difficult type, just to give you more practice. Usually there are only one or two questions on this section that contain such subtle distinctions that you're unable to answer confidently. And you then may find yourself stuck deciding between two possible choices, neither of which you're sure about.

EXAMINATION SECTION
TEST 1

DIRECTIONS: Each question consists of several sentences which can be arranged in a logical sequence. For each question, select the choice which places the numbered sentences in the MOST logical sequence. *PRINT THE LETTER OF THE CORRECT ANSWER IN THE SPACE AT THE RIGHT.*

1.
   I. A body was found in the woods.
   II. A man proclaimed innocence.
   III. The owner of a gun was located.
   IV. A gun was traced.
   V. The owner of a gun was questioned.
   The CORRECT answer is:
   A. IV, III, V, II, I
   B. II, I, IV, III, V
   C. I, IV, III, V, II
   D. I, III, V, II, IV
   E. I, II, IV, III, V

   1.____

2.
   I. A man is in a hunting accident.
   II. A man fell down a flight of steps.
   III. A man lost his vision in one eye.
   IV. A man broke his leg.
   V. A man had to walk with a cane.
   The CORRECT answer is:
   A. II, IV, V, I, III
   B. IV, V, I, III, II
   C. III, I, IV, V, II
   D. I, III, V, II, IV
   E. I, III, II, IV, V

   2.____

3.
   I. A man is offered a new job.
   II. A woman is offered a new job.
   III. A man works as a waiter.
   IV. A woman works as a waitress.
   V. A woman gives notice.
   The CORRECT answer is:
   A. IV, II, V, III, I
   B. IV, II, V, I, III
   C. II, IV, V, III, I
   D. III, I, IV, II, V
   E. IV, III, II, V, I

   3.____

4.
   I. A train let the station late.
   II. A man was late for work.
   III. A man lost his job.
   IV. Many people complained because the train was late.
   V. There was a traffic jam.
   The CORRECT answer is:
   A. V, II, I, IV, III
   B. V, I, IV, II, III
   C. V, I, II, IV, III
   D. I, V, IV, II, III
   E. II, I, IV, V, III

   4.____

115

5.
I. The burden of proof as to each issue is determined before trial and remains upon the same party throughout the trial.
II. The jury is at liberty to believe one witness' testimony as against a number of contradictory witnesses.
III. In a civil case, the party bearing the burden of proof is required to prove his contention by a fair preponderance of the evidence.
IV. However, it must be noted that a fair preponderance of evidence does not necessarily mean a greater number of witnesses.
V. The burden of proof is the burden which rests upon one of the parties to an action to persuade the trier of the facts, generally the jury, that a proposition he asserts is true.
VI. If the evidence is equally balanced, or if it leaves the jury in such doubt as to be unable to decide the controversy either way, judgment must be given against the party upon whom the burden of proof rests.
The CORRECT answer is:
A. III, II, V, IV, I, VI B. I, II, VI, V, III, IV C. III, IV, V, I, II, VI
D. V, I, III, VI, IV, II E. I, V, III, VI, IV, II

6.
I. If a parent is without assets and is unemployed, he cannot be convicted of the crime of non-support of a child.
II. The term *sufficient ability* has been held to mean sufficient financial ability.
III. It does not matter if his unemployment is by choice or unavoidable circumstances.
IV. If he fails to take any steps at all, he may be liable to prosecution for endangering the welfare of a child.
V. Under the penal law, a parent is responsible for the support of his minor child only if the parent is of *sufficient ability*.
VI. An indigent parent may meet his obligation by borrowing money or by seeking aid under the provisions of the Social Welfare Law.
The CORRECT answer is:
A. VI, I, V, III, II, IV B. I, III, V, II, IV, VI C. V, II, I, III, VI, IV
D. I, VI, IV, V, II, III E. II, V, I, III, VI, IV

7.
I. Consider, for example, the case of a rabble rouser who urges a group of twenty people to go out and break the windows of a nearby factory.
II. Therefore, the law fills the indicated gap with the crime of *inciting to riot*.
III. A person is considered guilty of inciting to riot when he urges ten or more persons to engage in tumultuous and violent conduct of a kind likely to create public alarm.
IV. However, if he has not obtained the cooperation of at least four people, he cannot be charged with unlawful assembly.
V. The charge of inciting to riot was added to the law to cover types of conduct which cannot be classified as either the crime of *riot* or the crime of *unlawful assembly*.
VI. If he acquires the acquiescence of at least four of them, he is guilty of unlawful assembly even if the project does not materialize.
The CORRECT answer is:
A. III, V, I, VI, IV, II B. V, I, IV, VI, II, III C. III, IV, I, V, II, VI
D. V, I, IV, VI, III, II E. V, III, I, VI, IV, II

8. I. If, however, the rebuttal evidence presents an issue of credibility, it is for the jury to determine whether the presumption has, in fact, been destroyed.
    II. Once sufficient evidence to the contrary is introduced, the presumption disappears from the trial.
    III. The effect of a presumption is to place the burden upon the adversary to come forward with evidence to rebut the presumption.
    IV. When a presumption is overcome and ceases to exist in the case, the fact or facts which gave rise to the presumption still remain.
    V. Whether a presumption has been overcome is ordinarily a question for the court.
    VI. Such information may furnish a basis for a logical inference.
    The CORRECT answer is:
    A. IV, VI, II, V, I, III   B. III, II, V, I, IV, VI   C. V, III, VI, IV, II, I
    D. V, IV, I, II, VI, III   E. II, III, V, I, IV, VI

9. I. An executive may answer a letter by writing his reply on the face of the letter itself instead of having a return letter typed.
    II. This procedure is efficient because it saves the executive's time, the typist's time, and saves office file space.
    III. Copying machines are used in small offices as well as large offices to save time and money in making brief replies to business letters.
    IV. A copy is made on a copying machine to go into the company files, while the original is mailed back to the sender.
    The CORRECT answer is:
    A. I, II, IV, III   B. I, IV, II, III   C. III, I, IV, II   D. III, IV, II, I

10. I. Most organizations favor one of the types but always include the others to a lesser degree.
    II. However, we can detect a definite trend toward greater use of symbolic control.
    III. We suggest that our local police agencies are today primarily utilizing material control.
    IV. Control can be classified into three types: physical, material, and symbolic.
    The CORRECT answer is:
    A. IV, II, III, I   B. II, I, IV, III   C. III, IV, II, I   D. IV, I, III, II

11. I. Project residents had first claim to this use, followed by surrounding neighborhood children.
    II. By contrast, recreation space within the project's interior was found to be used more often by both groups.
    III. Studies of the use of project grounds in many cities showed grounds left open for public use were neglected and unused, both by residents and by members of the surrounding community.
    IV. Project residents had clearly laid claim to the play spaces, setting up and enforcing unwritten rules for use.
    V. Each group, by experience, found their activities easily disrupted by other groups, and their claim to the use of space for recreation difficult to enforce.

The CORRECT answer is:
A. IV, V, I, II, III
B. V, II, IV, III, I
C. I, IV, III, II, V
D. III, V, II, IV, I

12. I. They do not consider the problems correctable within the existing subsidy formula and social policy of accepting all eligible applicants regardless of social behavior.
    II. A recent survey, however, indicated that tenants believe these problems correctable by local housing authorities and management within the existing financial formula.
    III. Many of the problems and complaints concerning public housing management and design have created resentment between the tenant and the landlord.
    IV. This same survey indicated that administrators and managers do not agree with the tenants.
    The CORRECT answer is:
    A. II, I, III, IV   B. I, III, IV, II   C. III, II, IV, I   D. IV, II, I, III

13. I. In single-family residences, there is usually enough distance between tenants to prevent occupants from annoying one another.
    II. For example, a certain small percentage of tenant families has one or more members addicted to alcohol.
    III. While managers believe in the right of individuals to live as they choose, the manager becomes concerned when the pattern of living jeopardizes others' rights.
    IV. Still others turn night into day, staging lusty entertainments which carry on into the hours when most tenants are trying to sleep.
    V. In apartment buildings, however, tenants live so closely together that any misbehavior can result in unpleasant living conditions.
    VI. Other families engage in violent argument.
    The CORRECT answer is:
    A. III, II, V, IV, VI, I
    B. I, V, II, VI, IV, III
    C. II, V, IV, I, III, VI
    D. IV, II, V, VI, III, I

14. I. Congress made the commitment explicit in the Housing Act of 194, establishing as a national goal the realization of a *decent home and suitable environment for every American family*.
    II. The result has been that the goal of decent home and suitable environment is still as far distant as ever for the disadvantaged urban family.
    III. In spite of this action by Congress, federal housing programs have continued to be fragmented and grossly underfunded.
    IV. The passage of the National Housing Act signaled a few federal commitment to provide housing for the nation's citizens.
    The CORRECT answer is:
    A. I, IV, III, II   B. IV, I, III, II   C. IV, I, II, III   D. II, IV, I, III

15. I. The greater expense does not necessarily involve *exploitation*, but it is often perceived as exploitative and unfair by those who are aware of the price differences involved, but unaware of operating costs.
    II. Ghetto residents believe they are *exploited* by local merchants, and evidence substantiates some of these beliefs.
    III. However, stores in low-income areas were more likely to be small independents, which could not achieve the economies available to supermarket chains and were, therefore, more likely to charge higher prices, and the customers were more likely to buy smaller-sized packages which are more expensive per unit of measure.
    IV. A study conducted in one city showed that distinctly higher prices were charged for goods sold in ghetto stores in other areas.
    The CORRECT answer is:
    A. IV, II, I, III   B. IV, I, III, II   C. II, IV, III, I   D. II, III, IV, I

15.____

KEY (CORRECT ANSWERS)

1.	C	6.	C	11.	D
2.	E	7.	A	12.	C
3.	B	8.	B	13.	B
4.	B	9.	C	14.	B
5.	D	10.	D	15.	C

120

PREPARING WRITTEN MATERIAL

EXAMINATION SECTION

TEST 1

DIRECTIONS: Each question or incomplete statement is followed by several suggested answers or completions. Select the one that BEST answers the question or completes the statement. *PRINT THE LETTER OF THE CORRECT ANSWER IN THE SPACE AT THE RIGHT.*

1. The one of the following sentences which is LEAST acceptable from the viewpoint of correct usage is:
   A. The police thought the fugitive to be him.
   B. The criminals set a trap for whoever would fall into it.
   C. It is ten years ago since the fugitive fled from the city.
   D. The lecturer argued that criminals are usually cowards.
   E. The police removed four bucketfuls of earth from the scene of the crime.

1.____

2. The one of the following sentences which is LEAST acceptable from the viewpoint of correct usage is:
   A. The patrolman scrutinized the report with great care.
   B. Approaching the victim of the assault, two bruises were noticed by the patrolman.
   C. As soon as I had broken down the door, I stepped into the room.
   D. I observed the accused loitering near the building, which was closed at the time.
   E. The storekeeper complained that his neighbor was guilty of violating a local ordinance.

2.____

3. The one of the following sentences which is LEAST acceptable from the viewpoint of correct usage is:
   A. I realized immediately that he intended to assault the woman, so I disarmed him.
   B. It was apparent that Mr. Smith's explanation contained many inconsistencies.
   C. Despite the slippery condition of the street, he managed to stop the vehicle before injuring the child.
   D. Not a single one of them wish, despite the damage to property, to make a formal complaint.
   E. The body was found lying on the floor.

3.____

4. The one of the following sentences which contains NO error in usage is:
   A. After the robbers left, the proprietor stood tied in his chair for about two hours before help arrived.
   B. In the cellar I found the watchman's hat and coat.
   C. The persons living in adjacent apartments stated that they had heard no unusual noises.

4.____

D. Neither a knife or any firearms were found in the room.
E. Walking down the street, the shouting of the crowd indicated that something was wrong.

5. The one of the following sentences which contains NO error in usage is:
   A. The policeman lay a firm hand on the suspect's shoulder.
   B. It is true that neither strength nor agility are the most important requirement for a good patrolman.
   C. Good citizens constantly strive to do more than merely comply the restraints imposed by society.
   D. No decision was made as to whom the prize should be awarded.
   E. Twenty years is considered a severe sentence for a felony.

6. Which of the following sentences is NOT expressed in standard English usage?
   A. The victim reached a pay-phone booth and manages to call police headquarters.
   B. By the time the call was received, the assailant had left the scene.
   C. The victim has been a respected member of the community for the past eleven years.
   D. Although the lighting was bad and the shadows were deep, the storekeeper caught sight of the attacker.
   E. Additional street lights have since been installed, and the patrols have been strengthened.

7. Which of the following sentences is NOT expressed in standard English usage?
   A. The judge upheld the attorney's right to question the witness about the missing glove.
   B. To be absolutely fair to all parties is the jury's chief responsibility.
   C. Having finished the report, a loud noise in the next room startled the sergeant.
   D. The witness obviously enjoyed having played a part in the proceedings.
   E. The sergeant planned to assign the case to whoever arrived first.

8. In which of the following sentences is a word misused?
   A. As a matter of principle, the captain insisted that the suspect's partner be brought for questioning.
   B. The principle suspect had been detained at the station house for most of the day.
   C. The principal in the crime had no previous criminal record, but his closest associate had been convicted of felonies on two occasions.
   D. The interest payments had been made promptly, but the firm had been drawing upon the principal for these payments.
   E. The accused insisted that his high school principal would furnish him a character reference.

9. Which of the following statements is ambiguous?
   A. Mr. Sullivan explained why Mr. Johnson had been dismissed from his job.
   B. The storekeeper told the patrolman he had made a mistake.
   C. After waiting three hours, the patients in the doctor's office were sent home.
   D. The janitor's duties were to maintain the building in good shape and to answer tenants' complaints.
   E. The speed limit should, in my opinion, be raised to sixty miles an hour on that stretch of road.

10. In which of the following is the punctuation or capitalization faulty?
    A. The accident occurred at an intersection in the Kew Gardens section of Queens, near the bus stop.
    B. The sedan, not the convertible, was struck in the side.
    C. Before any of the patrolmen had left the police car received an important message from headquarters.
    D. The dog that had been stolen was returned to his master, John Dempsey, who lived in East Village.
    E. The letter had been sent to 12 Hillside Terrace, Rutland, Vermont 05702.

Questions 11-25.

DIRECTIONS: Questions 11 through 25 are to be answered in accordance with correct English usage; that is, standard English rather than nonstandard or substandard. Nonstandard and substandard English includes words or expressions usually classified as slang, dialect, illiterate, etc., which are not generally accepted as correct in current written communication. Standard English also requires clarity, proper punctuation and capitalization and appropriate use of words. Write the letter of the sentence NOT expressed in standard English usage in the space at the right.

11. A. There were three witnesses to the accident.
    B. At least three witnesses were found to testify for the plaintiff.
    C. Three of the witnesses who took the stand was uncertain about the defendant's competence to drive.
    D. Only three witnesses came forward to testify for the plaintiff.
    E. The three witnesses to the accident were pedestrians.

12. A. The driver had obviously drunk too many martinis before leaving for home.
    B. The boy who drowned had swum in these same waters many times before.
    C. The petty thief had stolen a bicycle from a private driveway before he was apprehended.
    D. The detectives had brung in the heroin shipment they intercepted.
    E. The passengers had never ridden in a converted bus before.

13. A. Between you and me, the new platoon plan sounds like a good idea.
    B. Money from an aunt's estate was left to his wife and he.
    C. He and I were assigned to the same patrol for the first time in two months.
    D. Either you or he should check the front door of that store.
    E. The captain himself was not sure of the witness's reliability.

14. A. The alarm had scarcely begun to ring when the explosion occurred.
    B. Before the firemen arrived at the scene, the second story had been destroyed.
    C. Because of the dense smoke and heat, the firemen could hardly approach the now-blazing structure.
    D. According to the patrolman's report, there wasn't nobody in the store when the explosion occurred.
    E. The sergeant's suggestion was not at all unsound, but no one agreed with him.

15. A. The driver and the passenger they were both found to be intoxicated.
    B. The driver and the passenger talked slowly and not too clearly.
    C. Neither the driver nor his passengers were able to give a coherent account of the accident.
    D. In a corner of the room sat the passenger, quietly dozing.
    E. the driver finally told a strange and unbelievable story, which the passenger contradicted.

16. A. Under the circumstances I decided not to continue my examination of the premises.
    B. There are many difficulties now not comparable with those existing in 1960.
    C. Friends of the accused were heard to announce that the witness had better been away on the day of the trial.
    D. The two criminals escaped in the confusion that followed the explosion.
    E. The aged man was struck by the considerateness of the patrolman's offer.

17. A. An assemblage of miscellaneous weapons lay on the table.
    B. Ample opportunities were given to the defendant to obtain counsel.
    C. The speaker often alluded to his past experience with youthful offenders in the armed forces.
    D. The sudden appearance of the truck aroused my suspicions.
    E. Her studying had a good affect on her grades in high school.

18. A. He sat down in the theater and began to watch the movie.
    B. The girl had ridden horses since she was four years old.
    C. Application was made on behalf of the prosecutor to cite the witness for contempt.
    D. The bank robber, with his two accomplices, were caught in the act.
    E. His story is simply not credible.

19. A. The angry boy said that he did not like those kind of friends.
     B. The merchant's financial condition was so precarious that he felt he must avail himself of any offer of assistance.
     C. He is apt to promise more than he can perform.
     D. Looking at the messy kitchen, the housewife felt like crying.
     E. A clerk was left in charge of the stolen property.

20. A. His wounds were aggravated by prolonged exposure to sub-freezing temperatures.
     B. The prosecutor remarked that the witness was not averse to changing his story each time he was interviewed.
     C. The crime pattern indicated that the burglars were adapt in the handling of explosives.
     D. His rigid adherence to a fixed plan brought him into renewed conflict with his subordinates.
     E. He had anticipated that the sentence would be delivered by noon.

21. A. The whole arraignment procedure is badly in need of revision.
     B. After his glasses were broken in the fight, he would of gone to the optometrist if he could.
     C. Neither Tom nor Jack brought his lunch to work.
     D. He stood aside until the quarrel was over.
     E. A statement in the psychiatrist's report disclosed that the probationer vowed to have his revenge.

22. A. His fiery and intemperate speech to the striking employees fatally affected any chance of a future reconciliation.
     B. The wording of the statute has been variously construed.
     C. The defendant's attorney, speaking in the courtroom, called the official a demagogue who contempuously disregarded the judge's orders.
     D. The baseball game is likely to be the most exciting one this year.
     E. The mother divided the cookies among her two children.

23. A. There was only a bed and a dresser in the dingy room.
     B. John was one of the few students that have protested the new rule.
     C. It cannot be argued that the child's testimony is negligible; it is, on the contrary, of the greatest importance.
     D. The basic criterion for clearance was so general that officials resolved any doubts in favor of dismissal.
     E. Having just returned from a long vacation, the officer found the city unbearably hot.

24. A. The librarian ought to give more help to small children.
     B. The small boy was criticized by the teacher because he often wrote careless.
     C. It was generally doubted whether the women would permit the use of her apartment for intelligence operations.
     D. The probationer acts differently every time the officer visits him.
     E. Each of the newly appointed officers has 12 years of service.

25. A. The North is the most industrialized region in the country.
    B. L. Patrick Gray 3d, the bureau's acting director, stated that, while "rehabilitation is fine" for some convicted criminals, "it is a useless gesture for those who resist every such effort."
    C. Careless driving, faulty mechanism, narrow or badly kept roads all play their part in causing accidents.
    D. The childrens' books were left in the bus.
    E. It was a matter of internal security; consequently, he felt no inclination to rescind his previous order.

25.____

KEY (CORRECT ANSWERS)

1.	C	11.	C
2.	B	12.	D
3.	D	13.	B
4.	C	14.	D
5.	E	15.	A
6.	A	16.	C
7.	C	17.	E
8.	B	18.	D
9.	B	19.	A
10.	C	20.	C

21.	B
22.	E
23.	B
24.	B
25.	D

TEST 2

DIRECTIONS: Each question or incomplete statement is followed by several suggested answers or completions. Select the one that BEST answers the question or completes the statement. *PRINT THE LETTER OF THE CORRECT ANSWER IN THE SPACE AT THE RIGHT.*

Questions 1-6.

DIRECTIONS: Each of Questions 1 through 6 consists of a statement which contains a word (one of those underlined) that is either incorrectly used because it is not in keeping with the meaning the quotation is evidently intended to convey, or is misspelled. There is only one INCORRECT word in each quotation. Of the four underlined words, determine if the first one should be replaced by the word lettered A, the second replaced by the word lettered B, the third replaced by the word lettered C, or the fourth replaced by the word lettered D.

1. Whether one depends on fluorescent or artificial light or both, adequate standards should be maintained by means of systematic tests.
   A. natural   B. safeguards   C. established   D. routine

1.____

2. A police officer has to be prepared to assume his knowledge as a social scientist in the community.
   A. forced   B. role   C. philosopher   D. street

2.____

3. It is practically impossible to indicate whether a sentence is too long simply by measuring its length.
   A. almost   B. tell   C. very   D. guessing

3.____

4. Strong leaders are required to organize a community for delinquency prevention and for dissemination of organized crime and drug addiction.
   A. tactics   B. important   C. control   D. meetings

4.____

5. The demonstrators who were taken to the Criminal Courts building in Manhattan (because it was large enough to accommodate them), contended that the arrests were unwarranted.
   A. demonstraters   B. Manhatten
   C. accomodate   D. unwarranted

5.____

6. They were guaranteed a calm atmosphere, free from harassment, which would be conducive to quiet consideration of the indictments.
   A. guarenteed   B. atmspher
   C. harassment   D. inditements

6.____

Questions 7-11.

DIRECTIONS: Each of Questions 7 through 11 consists of a statement containing four words in capital letters. One of these words in capital letters is not in keeping with the meaning which the statement is evidently intended to carry. The four words in capital letters in each statement are reprinted after the statement. Print the capital letter preceding the one of the four words which does MOST to spoil the true meaning of the statement in the space at the right.

7. Retirement and pension systems are essential not only to provide employees with with a means of support in the future, but also to prevent longevity and CHARITABLE considerations from UPSETTING the PROMOTIONAL opportunities RETIRED members of the career service. 7.____
   A. charitable   B. upsetting   C. promotional   D. retired

8. Within each major DIVISION in a properly set up public or private organization, provision is made so that each NECESSARY activity is CARED for and lines of authority and responsibility are clear-cut and INFINITE. 8.____
   A. division   B. necessary   C. cared   D. infinite

9. In public service, the scale of salaries paid must be INCIDENTAL to the services rendered, with due CONSIDERATION for the attraction of the desired MANPOWER and for the maintenance of a standard of living COMMENSURATE with the work to be performed. 9.____
   A. incidental   B. consideration
   C. manpower   D. commensurate

10. An understanding of the AIMS of an organization by the staff will AID greatly in increasing the DEMAND of the correspondence work of the office, and will to a large extent DETERMINE the nature of the correspondence. 10.____
    A. aims   B. aid   C. demand   D. determine

11. BECAUSE the Civil Service Commission strongly feels that the MERIT system is a key factor in the MAINTENANCE of democratic government, it has adopted as one of its major DEFENSES the progressive democratization of its own procedures in dealing with candidates for positions in the public service. 11.____
    A. Because   B. merit   C. maintenance   D. defenses

Questions 12-14.

DIRECTIONS: Questions 12 through 14 consist of one sentence each. Each sentence contains an incorrectly used word. First, decide which is the incorrectly used word. Then, from among the options given, decide which word, when substituted for the incorrectly used word, makes the meaning of the sentence clear.
EXAMPLE:
The U.S. national income exhibits a pattern of long term deflection.
   A. reflection   B. subjection   C. rejoicing   D. growth

The word *deflection* in the sentence does not convey the meaning the sentence evidently intended to convey. The word *growth* (Answer D), when substituted for the word *deflection*, makes the meaning of the sentence clear. Accordingly, the answer to the question is D.

12. The study commissioned by the joint committee fell compassionately short of the mark and would have to be redone.
    A. successfully
    B. insignificantly
    C. experimentally
    D. woefully

13. He will not idly exploit any violation of the provisions of the order.
    A. tolerate B. refuse C. construe D. guard

14. The defendant refused to be virile and bitterly protested service.
    A. irked B. feasible C. docile D. credible

Questions 15-25.

DIRECTIONS: Questions 15 through 25 consist of short paragraphs. Each paragraph contains one word which is INCORRECTLY used because it is NOT in keeping with the meaning of the paragraph. Find the word in each paragraph which is INCORRECTLY used and then select as the answer the suggested word which should be substituted for the incorrectly used word.

SAMPLE QUESTION:
In determining who is to do the work in your unit, you will have to decide just who does what from day to day. One of your lowest responsibilities is to assign work so that everybody gets a fair share and that everyone can do his part well.
    A. new B. old C. important D. performance

EXPLANATION:
The word which is NOT in keeping with the meaning of the paragraph is *lowest*. This is the INCORRECTLY used word. The suggested word *important* would be in keeping with the meaning of the paragraph and should be substituted for *lowest*. Therefore, the CORRECT answer is choice C.

15. If really good practice in the elimination of preventable injuries is to be achieved and held in any establishment, top management must refuse full and definite responsibility and must apply a good share of its attention to the task.
    A. accept B. avoidable C. duties D. problem

16. Recording the human face for identification is by no means the only service performed by the camera in the field of investigation. When the trial of any issue takes place, a word picture is sought to be distorted to the court of incidents, occurrences, or events which are in dispute.
    A. appeals B. description C. portrayed D. deranged

17. In the collection of physical evidence, it cannot be emphasized too strongly that a haphazard systematic search at the scene of the crime is vital. Nothing must be overlooked. Often the only leads in a case will come from the results of this search.
    A. important
    B. investigation
    C. proof
    D. thorough

17.____

18. If an investigator has reason to suspect that the witness is mentally stable, or a habitual drunkard, he should leave no stone unturned in his investigation to determine if the witness was under the influence of liquor or drugs, or was mentally unbalanced either at the time of the occurrence to which he testified or at the time of the trial.
    A. accused
    B. clue
    C. deranged
    D. question

18.____

19. The use of records is a valuable step in crime investigation and is the main reason every department should maintain accurate reports. Crimes are not committed through the use of departmental records alone but from the use of all records, of almost every type, wherever they may be found and whenever they give any incidental information regarding the criminal.
    A. accidental
    B. necessary
    C. reported
    D. solved

19.____

20. In the years since passage of the Harrison Narcotic Act of 1914, making the possession of opium amphetamines illegal in most circumstances, drug use has become a subject of considerable scientific interest and investigation. There is at present a voluminous literature on drug use of various kinds.
    A. ingestion
    B. derivatives
    C. addiction
    D. opiates

20.____

21. Of course, the fact that criminal laws are extremely patterned in definition does not mean that the majority of persons who violate them are dealt with as criminals. Quite the contrary, for a great many forbidden acts are voluntarily engaged in within situations of privacy and go unobserved and unreported.
    A. symbolic
    B. casual
    C. scientific
    D. broad-gauged

21.____

22. The most punitive way to study punishment is to focus attention on the pattern of punitive action: to study how a penalty is applied, too study what is done to or taken from an offender.
    A. characteristic
    B. degrading
    C. objective
    D. distinguished

22.____

23. The most common forms of punishment in times past have been death, physical torture, mutilation, branding, public humiliation, fines, forfeits of property, banishment, transportation, and imprisonment. Although this list is by no means differentiated, practically every form of punishment has had several variations and applications.
    A. specific
    B. simple
    C. exhaustive
    D. characteristic

23.____

24. There is another important line of inference between ordinary and professional criminals, and that is the source from which they are recruited. The professional criminal seems to be drawn from legitimate employment and, in many instances, from parallel vocations or pursuits.
    A. demarcation   B. justification   C. superiority   D. reference

24.____

25. He took the position that the success of the program was insidious on getting additional revenue.
    A. reputed   B. contingent   C. failure   D. indeterminate

25.____

KEY (CORRECT ANSWERS)

1.	A		11.	D
2.	B		12.	D
3.	B		13.	A
4.	C		14.	C
5.	D		15.	A
6.	C		16.	C
7.	D		17.	D
8.	D		18.	C
9.	A		19.	D
10.	C		20.	B

21. D
22. C
23. C
24. A
25. B

TEST 3

DIRECTIONS: Each question or incomplete statement is followed by several suggested answers or completions. Select the one that BEST answers the question or completes the statement. *PRINT THE LETTER OF THE CORRECT ANSWER IN THE SPACE AT THE RIGHT.*

Questions 1-5.

DIRECTIONS: Questions 1 through 5 are to be answered on the basis of the following.

You are a supervising officer in an investigative unit. Earlier in the day, you directed Detectives Tom Dixon and Sal Mayo to investigate a reported assault and robbery in a liquor store within your area of jurisdiction.
Detective Dixon has submitted to you a preliminary investigative report containing the following information:

- At 1630 hours on 2/20, arrived at Joe's Liquor Store at 350 SW Avenue with Detective Mayo to investigate A & R.
- At store interviewed Rob Ladd, store manager, who stated that he and Joe Brown (store owner) had been stuck up about ten minutes prior to our arrival.
- Ladd described the robbers as male whites in their late teens or early twenties. Further stated that one of the robbers displayed what appeared to be an automatic pistol as he entered the store, and said, *Give us the money or we'll kill you.* Ladd stated that Brown then reached under the counter where he kept a loaded .38 caliber pistol. Several shots followed, and Ladd threw himself to the floor.
- The robbers fled, and Ladd didn't know if any money had been taken.
- At this point, Ladd realized that Brown was unconscious on the floor and bleeding from a head wound.
- Ambulance called by Ladd, and Brown was removed by same to General Hospital.
- Personally interviewed John White, 382 Dartmouth Place, who stated he was inside store at the time of occurrence. White states that he hid behind a wine display upon hearing someone say, *Give us the money.* He then heard shots and saw two young men run from the store to a yellow car parked at the curb. White was unable to further describe auto. States the taller of the two men drove the car away while the other sat on passenger side in front.
- Recovered three spent .38 caliber bullets from premises and delivered them to Crime Lab.
- To General Hospital at 1800 hours but unable to interview Brown, who was under sedation and suffering from shock and a laceration of the head.
- Alarm #12487 transmitted for car and occupants.
- Case Active.

Based solely on the contents of the preliminary investigation submitted by Detective Dixon, select one sentence from the following groups of sentences which is MOST accurate and is grammatically correct.

1. A. Both robbers were armed.
   B. Each of the robbers were described as a male white.
   C. Neither robber was armed.
   D. Mr. Ladd stated that one of the robbers was armed.

2. A. Mr. Brown fired three shots from his revolver.
   B. Mr. Brown was shot in the head by one of the robbers.
   C. Mr. Brown suffered a gunshot wound of the head during the course of the robbery.
   D. Mr. Brown was taken to General Hospital by ambulance.

3. A. Shots were fired after one of the robbers said, *Give us the money or we'll kill you.*
   B. After one of the robbers demanded the money from Mr. Brown, he fired a shot.
   C. The preliminary investigation indicated that although Mr. Brown did not have a license for the gun, he was justified in using deadly physical force.
   D. Mr. Brown was interviewed at General Hospital.

4. A. Each of the witnesses were customers in the store at the time of occurrence.
   B. Neither of the witnesses interviewed was the owner of the liquor store.
   C. Neither of the witnesses interviewed were the owner of the store.
   D. Neither of the witnesses was employed by Mr. Brown.

5. A. Mr. Brown arrived at General Hospital at about 5:00 P.M.
   B. Neither of the robbers was injured during the robbery.
   C. The robbery occurred at 3:30 P.M. on February 10.
   D. One of the witnesses called the ambulance.

Questions 6-10.

DIRECTIONS: Each of Questions 6 through 10 consists of information given in outline form and four sentences labeled A, B, C, and D. For each question, choose the one sentence which CORRECTLY expresses the information given in outline form and which also displays PROPER English usage.

6. Client's Name: Joanna Jones
   Number of Children: 3
   Client's Income: None
   Client's Marital Status: Single

   A. Joanna Jones is an unmarried client with three children who have no income.
   B. Joanna Jones, who is single and has no income, a client she has three children.
   C. Joanna Jones, whose three children are clients, is single and has no income.
   D. Joanna Jones, who has three children, is an unmarried client with no income.

7. Client's Name: Bertha Smith   7.____
   Number of Children: 2
   Client's Rent: $1050 per month
   Number of Rooms: 4

   A. Bertha Smith, a client, pays $1050 per month for her four rooms with two children.
   B. Client Bertha Smith has two children and pays $1050 per month for four rooms.
   C. Client Bertha Smith is paying $1050 per month for two children with four rooms.
   D. For four rooms and two children client Bertha Smith pays $1050 per month.

8. Name of Employee: Cynthia Dawes   8.____
   Number of Cases Assigned: 9
   Date Cases were Assigned: 12/16
   Number of Assigned Cases Completed: 8

   A. On December 16, employee Cynthia Dawes was assigned nine cases; she has completed eight of these cases.
   B. Cynthia Dawes, employee on December 16, assigned nine cases, completed eight.
   C. Being employed on December 16, Cynthia Dawes completed eight of nine assigned cases.
   D. Employee Cynthia Dawes, she was assigned nine cases and completed eight, on December 16.

9. Place of Audit: Broadway Center   9.____
   Names of Auditors: Paul Cahn, Raymond Perez
   Date of Audit: 11/20
   Number of Cases Audited: 41

   A. On November 20, at the Broadway Center 41 cases was audited by auditors Paul Cahn and Raymond Perez.
   B. Auditors Raymond Perez and Paul Cahn has audited 41 cases at the Broadway Center on November 20.
   C. At the Broadway Center, on November 20, auditors Paul Cahn and Raymond Perez audited 41 cases.
   D. Auditors Paul Cahn and Raymond Perez at the Broadway Center, on November 20, is auditing 41 cases.

10. Name of Client: Barbra Levine   10.____
    Client's Monthly Income: $2100
    Client's Monthly Expenses: $4520

    A. Barbra Levine is a client, her monthly income is $2100 and her monthly expenses is $4520.
    B. Barbra Levine's monthly income is $2100 and she is a client, with whose monthly expenses are $4520.

C. Barbra Levine is a client whose monthly income is $2100 and whose monthly expenses are $4520.
D. Barbra Levine, a client, is with a monthly income which is $2100 and monthly expenses which are $4520.

Questions 11-13.

DIRECTIONS: Questions 11 through 13 involve several statements of fact presented in a very simple way. These statements of fact are followed by 4 choices which attempt to incorporate all of the facts into one logical statement which is properly constructed and grammatically correct.

11. I. Mr. Brown was sweeping the sidewalk in front of his house.
    II. He was sweeping it because it was dirty.
    III. He swept the refuse into the street.
    IV. Police Officer gave him a ticket.

    Which one of the following BEST presents the information given above?
    A. Because his sidewalk was dirty, Mr. Brown received a ticket from Officer Green when he swept the refuse into the street.
    B. Police Officer Green gave Mr. Brown a ticket because his sidewalk was dirty and he swept the refuse into the street.
    C. Police Officer Green gave Mr. Brown a ticket for sweeping refuse into the street because his sidewalk was dirty.
    D. Mr. Brown, who was sweeping refuse from his dirty sidewalk into the street, was given a ticket by Police Officer Green.

12. I. Sergeant Smith radioed for help.
    II. The sergeant did so because the crowd was getting larger.
    III. It was 10:00 A.M. when he made his call.
    IV. Sergeant Smith was not in uniform at the time of occurrence.

    Which one of the following BEST presents the information given above?
    A. Sergeant Smith, although not on duty at the time, radioed for help at 10 o'clock because the crowd was getting uglier.
    B. Although not in uniform, Sergeant Smith called for help at 10:00 A.M. because the crowd was getting uglier.
    C. Sergeant Smith radioed for help at 10:00 A.M. because the crowd was getting larger.
    D. Although he was not in uniform, Sergeant Smith radioed for help at 10:00 A.M. because the crowd was getting larger.

13. I. The payroll office is open on Fridays.
    II. Paychecks are distributed from 9:00 A.M. to 12 Noon.
    III. The office is open on Fridays because that's the only day the payroll staff is available.
    IV. It is open for the specified hours in order to permit employees to cash checks at the bank during lunch hour.

The choice below which MOST clearly and accurately presents the above idea is:
- A. Because the payroll office is open on Fridays from 9:00 A.M. to 12 Noon, employees can cash their checks when the payroll staff is available.
- B. Because the payroll staff is only available on Fridays until noon, employees can cash their checks during their lunch hour.
- C. Because the payroll staff is available only on Fridays, the office is open from 9:00 A.M. to 12 Noon to allow employees to cash their checks.
- D. Because of payroll staff availability, the payroll office is open on Fridays. It is open from 9:00 A.M. to 12 Noon so that distributed paychecks can be cashed at the bank while employees are on their lunch hour.

Questions 14-16.

DIRECTIONS: In each of Questions 14 through 6, the four sentences are from a paragraph in a report. They are not in the right order. Which of the following arrangements is the BEST one?

14.
  I. An executive may answer a letter by writing his reply on the face of the letter itself instead of having a return letter typed.
  II. This procedure is efficient because it saves the executive's time, the typist's time, and saves office file space.
  III. Copying machines are used in small offices as well as large offices to save time and money in making brief replies to business letters.
  IV. A copy is made on a copy machine to go into the company files, while the original is mailed back to the sender.

  The CORRECT answer is:
   A. I, II, IV, III   B. I, IV, II, III   C. III, I, IV, II   D. III, IV, II, I

15.
  I. Most organizations favor one of the types but always include the others to a lesser degree.
  II. However, we can detect a definite trend toward greater use of symbolic control.
  III. We suggest that our local police agencies are today primarily utilizing material control.
  IV. Control can be classified into three types: physical, material, and symbolic.

  The CORRECT answer is:
   A. IV, II, III, I   B. II, I, IV, III   C. III, IV, II, I   D. IV, I, III, II

16.
  I. They can and do take advantage of ancient political and geographical boundaries, which often give them sanctuary from effective policy activity.
  II. This country is essentially a country of small police forces, each operating independently within the limits of its jurisdiction.
  III. The boundaries that define and limit police operations do not hinder the movement of criminals, of course.
  IV. The machinery of law enforcement in America is fragmented, complicated, and frequently overlapping.

The CORRECT answer is:
A. III, I, IV   B. II, IV, I, III   C. IV, II, III, I   D. IV, III, II, I

17. Examine the following sentence, and then choose from below the words which should be inserted in the blank spaces to produce the best sentence.
The unit has exceeded _____ goals and the employees are satisfied with _____ accomplishments.
   A. their, it's   B. it's; it's   C. its, there   D. its, their

18. Examine the following sentence, and then choose from below the words which should be inserted in the blank spaces to produce the best sentence.
Research indicates that employees who _____ no opportunity for close social relationships often find their work unsatisfying, and this _____ of satisfaction often reflects itself in low production.
   A. have; lack   B. have; excess   C. has; lack   D. has; excess

19. Words in a sentence must be arranged properly to make sure that the intended meaning of the sentence is clear.
The sentence below that does NOT make sense because a clause has been separated from the word on which its meaning depends is:
   A. To be a good writer, clarity is necessary.
   B. To be a good writer, you must write clearly.
   C. You must write clearly to be a good writer.
   D. Clarity is necessary to good writing.

Questions 20-21.

DIRECTIONS: Each of Questions 20 and 21 consists of a statement which contains a word (one of those underlined) that is either incorrectly used because it is not in keeping with the meaning the quotation is evidently intended to convey, or is misspelled. There is only one INCORRECT word in each quotation. Of the four underlined words, determine if the first one should be replaced by the word lettered A, the second one replaced by the word lettered B, the third one replaced by the word lettered C, or the fourth one replaced by the word lettered D.

20. The alleged killer was occasionally permitted to excercise in the corridor.
   A. alledged   B. ocasionally   C. permited   D. exercise

21. Defense counsel stated, in affect, that their conduct was permissible under the First Amendment.
   A. council   B. effect   C. there   D. permissable

Question 22.

DIRECTIONS: Question 22 consists of one sentence. This sentence contains an incorrectly used word. First, decide which is the incorrectly used word. Then, from among the options given, decide which word, when substituted for the incorrectly used word, makes the meaning of the sentence clear.

22. As today's violence has no single cause, so its causes have no single scheme. 22.____
    A. deference   B. cure   C. flaw   D. relevance

23. In the sentence, *A man in a light-grey suit waited thirty-five minutes in the ante-room for the all-important document*, the word IMPROPERLY hyphenated is 23.____
    A. light-grey
    B. thirty-five
    C. ante-room
    D. all-important

24. In the sentence, *The candidate wants to file his application for preference before it is too late*, the word *before* is used as a(n) 24.____
    A. preposition
    B. subordinating conjunction
    C. pronoun
    D. adverb

25. In the sentence, *The perpetrators ran from the scene*, the word *from* is a 25.____
    A. preposition   B. pronoun   C. verb   D. conjunction

KEY (CORRECT ANSWERS)

1.	D		11.	D
2.	D		12.	D
3.	A		13.	D
4.	B		14.	C
5.	D		15.	D
6.	D		16.	C
7.	B		17.	D
8.	A		18.	A
9.	C		19.	A
10.	C		20.	D

21.	B
22.	B
23.	C
24.	B
25.	A

PHILOSOPHY, PRINCIPLES, PRACTICES, AND TECHNICS OF SUPERVISION, ADMINISTRATION, MANAGEMENT, AND ORGANIZATION

TABLE OF CONTENTS

	Page
MEANING OF SUPERVISION	1
THE OLD AND THE NEW SUPERVISION	1
THE EIGHT (8) BASIC PRINCIPLES OF THE NEW SUPERVISION	1
I. Principle of Responsibility	1
II. Principle of Authority	2
III. Principle of Self-Growth	2
IV. Principle of Individual Worth	2
V. Principle of Creative Leadership	2
VI. Principle of Success and Failure	2
VII. Principle of Science	3
VIII. Principle of Cooperation	3
WHAT IS ADMINISTRATION?	3
I. Practices Commonly Classed as "Supervisory"	3
II. Practices Commonly Classed as "Administrative"	3
III. Practices Commonly Classed as Both "Supervisory" and "Administrative"	4
RESPONSIBILITIES OF THE SUPERVISOR	4
COMPETENCIES OF THE SUPERVISOR	4
THE PROFESSIONAL SUPERVISOR-EMPLOYEE RELATIONSHIP	4
MINI-TEXT IN SUPERVISION, ADMINISTRATION, MANAGEMENT, AND ORGANIZATION	5
I. Brief Highlights	5
A. Levels of Management	6
B. What the Supervisor Must Learn	6
C. A Definition of Supervision	6
D. Elements of the Team Concept	6
E. Principles of Organization	6
F. The Four Important Parts of Every Job	7
G. Principles of Delegation	7
H. Principles of Effective Communications	7
I. Principles of Work Improvement	7
J. Areas of Job Improvement	7
K. Seven Key Points in Making Improvements	8

	L.	Corrective Techniques for Job Improvement	8
	M.	A Planning Checklist	8
	N.	Five Characteristics of Good Directions	9
	O.	Types of Directions	9
	P.	Controls	9
	Q.	Orienting the New Employee	9
	R.	Checklist for Orienting New Employees	9
	S.	Principles of Learning	10
	T.	Causes of Poor Performance	10
	U.	Four Major Steps in On-the-Job Instructions	10
	V.	Employees Want Five Things	10
	W.	Some Don'ts in Regard to Praise	11
	X.	How to Gain Your Workers' Confidence	11
	Y.	Sources of Employee Problems	11
	Z.	The Supervisor's Key to Discipline	11
	AA.	Five Important Processes of Management	12
	BB.	When the Supervisor Fails to Plan	12
	CC.	Fourteen General Principles of Management	12
	DD.	Change	12
II.	Brief Topical Summaries		13
	A.	Who/What is the Supervisor?	13
	B.	The Sociology of Work	13
	C.	Principles and Practices of Supervision	14
	D.	Dynamic Leadership	14
	E.	Processes for Solving Problems	15
	F.	Training for Results	15
	G.	Health, Safety, and Accident Prevention	16
	H.	Equal Employment Opportunity	16
	I.	Improving Communications	16
	J.	Self-Development	17
	K.	Teaching and Training	17
		1. The Teaching Process	17
		a. Preparation	17
		b. Presentation	18
		c. Summary	18
		d. Application	18
		e. Evaluation	18
		2. Teaching Methods	18
		a. Lecture	18
		b. Discussion	18
		c. Demonstration	19
		d. Performance	19
		e. Which Method to Use	19

PHILOSOPHY, PRINCIPLES, PRACTICES, AND TECHNICS
OF
SUPERVISION, ADMINISTRATION, MANAGEMENT, AND ORGANIZATION

MEANING OF SUPERVISION

The extension of the democratic philosophy has been accompanied by an extension in the scope of supervision. Modern leaders and supervisors no longer think of supervision in the narrow sense of being confined chiefly to visiting employees, supplying materials, or rating the staff. They regard supervision as being intimately related to all the concerned agencies of society, they speak of the supervisor's function in terms of "growth," rather than the "improvement" of employees.

This modern concept of supervision may be defined as follows: Supervision is leadership and the development of leadership within groups which are cooperatively engaged in inspection, research, training, guidance, and evaluation.

THE OLD AND THE NEW SUPERVISION

TRADITIONAL
1. Inspection
2. Focused on the employee
3. Visitation
4. Random and haphazard
5. Imposed and authoritarian
6. One person usually

MODERN
1. Study and analysis
2. Focused on aims, materials, methods, supervisors, employees, environment
3. Demonstrations, intervisitation, workshops, directed reading, bulletins, etc.
4. Definitely organized and planned (scientific)
5. Cooperative and democratic
6. Many persons involved (creative)

THE EIGHT (8) BASIC PRINCIPLES OF THE NEW SUPERVISION

I. Principle of Responsibility
   Authority to act and responsibility for acting must be joined.
   A. If you give responsibility, give authority.
   B. Define employee duties clearly.
   C. Protect employees from criticism by others.
   D. Recognize the rights as well as obligations of employees.
   E. Achieve the aims of a democratic society insofar as it is possible within the area of your work.
   F. Establish a situation favorable to training and learning.
   G. Accept ultimate responsibility for everything done in your section, unit, office, division, department.
   H. Good administration and good supervision are inseparable.

II. Principle of Authority
The success of the supervisor is measured by the extent to which the power of authority is not used.
   A. Exercise simplicity and informality in supervision
   B. Use the simplest machinery of supervision
   C. If it is good for the organization as a whole, it is probably justified.
   D. Seldom be arbitrary or authoritative.
   E. Do not base your work on the power of position or of personality.
   F. Permit and encourage the free expression of opinions.

III. Principle of Self-Growth
The success of the supervisor is measured by the extent to which, and the speed with which, he is no longer needed.
   A. Base criticism on principles, not on specifics.
   B. Point out higher activities to employees.
   C. Train for self-thinking by employees to meet new situations.
   D. Stimulate initiative, self-reliance, and individual responsibility
   E. Concentrate on stimulating the growth of employees rather than on removing defects.

IV. Principle of Individual Worth
Respect for the individual is a paramount consideration in supervision.
   A. Be human and sympathetic in dealing with employees.
   B. Don't nag about things to be done.
   C. Recognize the individual differences among employees and seek opportunities to permit best expression of each personality.

V. Principle of Creative Leadership
The best supervision is that which is not apparent to the employee.
   A. Stimulate, don't drive employees to creative action.
   B. Emphasize doing good things.
   C. Encourage employees to do what they do best.
   D. Do not be too greatly concerned with details of subject or method.
   E. Do not be concerned exclusively with immediate problems and activities.
   F. Reveal higher activities and make them both desired and maximally possible.
   G. Determine procedures in the light of each situation but see that these are derived from a sound basic philosophy.
   H. Aid, inspire, and lead so as to liberate the creative spirit latent in all good employees.

VI. Principle of Success and Failure
There are no unsuccessful employees, only unsuccessful supervisors who have failed to give proper leadership.
   A. Adapt suggestions to the capacities, attitudes, and prejudices of employees.
   B. Be gradual, be progressive, be persistent.
   C. Help the employee find the general principle; have the employee apply his own problem to the general principle.
   D. Give adequate appreciation for good work and honest effort.
   E. Anticipate employee difficulties and help to prevent them.
   F. Encourage employees to do the desirable things they will do anyway.
   G. Judge your supervision by the results it secures.

VII. Principle of Science
Successful supervision is scientific, objective, and experimental. It is based on facts, not on prejudices.
- A. Be cumulative in results.
- B. Never divorce your suggestions from the goals of training.
- C. Don't be impatient of results.
- D. Keep all matters on a professional, not a personal, level.
- E. Do not be concerned exclusively with immediate problems and activities.
- F. Use objective means of determining achievement and rating where possible.

VIII. Principle of Cooperation
Supervision is a cooperative enterprise between supervisor and employee.
- A. Begin with conditions as they are.
- B. Ask opinions of all involved when formulating policies.
- C. Organization is as good as its weakest link.
- D. Let employees help to determine policies and department programs.
- E. Be approachable and accessible—physically and mentally.
- F. Develop pleasant social relationships.

WHAT IS ADMINISTRATION

Administration is concerned with providing the environment, the material facilities, and the operational procedures that will promote the maximum growth and development of supervisors and employees. (Organization is an aspect and a concomitant of administration.)

There is no sharp line of demarcation between supervision and administration; these functions are intimately interrelated and, often, overlapping. They are complementary activities.

I. Practices Commonly Classed as "Supervisory"
- A. Conducting employees' conferences
- B. Visiting sections, units, offices, divisions, departments
- C. Arranging for demonstrations
- D. Examining plans
- E. Suggesting professional reading
- F. Interpreting bulletins
- G. Recommending in-service training courses
- H. Encouraging experimentation
- I. Appraising employee morale
- J. Providing for intervisitation

II. Practices Commonly Classified as "Administrative"
- A. Management of the office
- B. Arrangement of schedules for extra duties
- C. Assignment of rooms or areas
- D. Distribution of supplies
- E. Keeping records and reports
- F. Care of audio-visual materials
- G. Keeping inventory records
- H. Checking record cards and books

      I.   Programming special activities
      J.   Checking on the attendance and punctuality of employees

III.   Practices Commonly Classified as Both "Supervisory" and "Administrative"
     A.   Program construction
     B.   Testing or evaluating outcomes
     C.   Personnel accounting
     D.   Ordering instructional materials

RESPONSIBILITIES OF THE SUPERVISOR

A person employed in a supervisory capacity must constantly be able to improve his own efficiency and ability. He represent the employer to the employees and only continuous self-examination can make him a capable supervisor.

Leadership and training are the supervisor's responsibility. An efficient working unit is one in which the employees work with the supervisor. It is his job to bring out the best in his employees. He must always be relaxed, courteous, and calm in his association with his employees. Their feelings are important, and a harsh attitude does not develop the most efficient employees.

COMPETENCES OF THE SUPERVISOR

    I.   Complete knowledge of the duties and responsibilities of his position.
    II.   To be able to organize a job, plan ahead, and carry through.
    III.   To have self-confidence and initiative.
    IV.   To be able to handle the unexpected situation and make quick decisions.
    V.   To be able to properly train subordinates in the positions they are best suited for.
    VI.   To be able to keep good human relations among his subordinates.
    VII. To be able to keep good human relations between his subordinates and himself and to earn their respect and trust.

THE PROFESSIONAL SUPERVISOR-EMPLOYEE RELATIONSHIP

There are two kinds of efficiency: one kind is only apparent and is produced in organizations through the exercise of mere discipline; this is but a simulation of the second, or true, efficiency which springs from spontaneous cooperation. If you are a manager, no matter how great or small your responsibility, it is your job, in the final analysis, to create and develop this involuntary cooperation among the people whom you supervise. For, no matter how powerful a combination of money, machines, and materials a company may have, this is a dead and sterile thing without a team of willing, thinking, and articulate people to guide it.

The following 21 points are presented as indicative of the exemplary basic relationship that should exist between supervisor and employee:

1. Each person wants to be liked and respected by his fellow employee and wants to be treated with consideration and respect by his superior.
2. The most competent employee will make an error. However, in a unit where good relations exist between the supervisor and his employees, tenseness and fear do not exist. Thus, errors are not hidden or covered up, and the efficiency of a unit is not impaired.

3. Subordinates resent rules, regulations, or orders that are unreasonable or unexplained.
4. Subordinates are quick to resent unfairness, harshness, injustices, and favoritism.
5. An employee will accept responsibility if he knows that he will be complimented for a job well done, and not too harshly chastised for failure; that his supervisor will check the cause of the failure, and, if it was the supervisor's fault, he will assume the blame therefore. If it was the employee's fault, his supervisor will explain the correct method or means of handling the responsibility.
6. An employee wants to receive credit for a suggestion he has made, that is used. If a suggestion cannot be used, the employee is entitled to an explanation. The supervisor should not say "no" and close the subject.
7. Fear and worry slow up a worker's ability. Poor working environment can impair his physical and mental health. A good supervisor avoids forceful methods, threats, and arguments to get a job done.
8. A forceful supervisor is able to train his employees individually and as a team, and is able to motivate them in the proper channels.
9. A mature supervisor is able to properly evaluate his subordinates and to keep them happy and satisfied.
10. A sensitive supervisor will never patronize his subordinates.
11. A worthy supervisor will respect his employees' confidences.
12. Definite and clear-cut responsibilities should be assigned to each executive.
13. Responsibility should always be coupled with corresponding authority.
14. No change should be made in the scope or responsibilities of a position without a definite understanding to that effect on the part of all persons concerned.
15. No executive or employee, occupying a single position in the organization, should be subject to definite orders from more than one source.
16. Orders should never be given to subordinates over the head of a responsible executive. Rather than do this, the officer in question should be supplanted.
17. Criticisms of subordinates should, whoever possible, be made privately, and in no case should a subordinate be criticized in the presence of executives or employees of equal or lower rank.
18. No dispute or difference between executives or employees as to authority or responsibilities should be considered too trivial for prompt and careful adjudication.
19. Promotions, wage changes, and disciplinary action should always be approved by the executive immediately superior to the one directly responsible.
20. No executive or employee should ever be required, or expected, to be at the same time an assistant to, and critic of, another.
21. Any executive whose work is subject to regular inspection should, wherever practicable, be given the assistance and facilities necessary to enable him to maintain an independent check of the quality of his work.

MINI-TEXT IN SUPERVISION, ADMINISTRATION, MANAGEMENT, AND ORGANIZATION

I. Brief Highlights

Listed concisely and sequentially are major headings and important data in the field for quick recall and review.

A. Levels of Management
Any organization of some size has several levels of management. In terms of a ladder, the levels are:

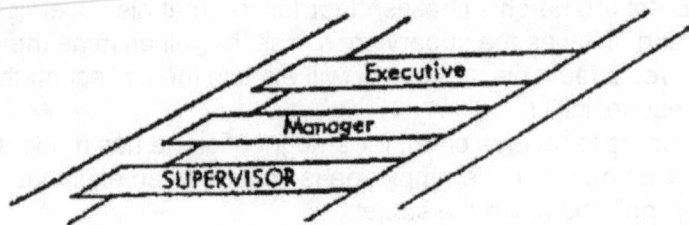

The first level is very important because it is the beginning point of management leadership.

B. What the Supervisor Must Learn
A supervisor must learn to:
1. Deal with people and their differences
2. Get the job done through people
3. Recognize the problems when they exist
4. Overcome obstacles to good performance
5. Evaluate the performance of people
6. Check his own performance in terms of accomplishment

C. A Definition of Supervisor
The term supervisor means any individual having authority, in the interests of the employer, to hire, transfer, suspend, lay-off, recall, promote, discharge, assign, reward, or discipline other employees or responsibility to direct them, or to adjust their grievances, or effectively to recommend such action, if, in connection with the foregoing, exercise of such authority is not of a merely routine or clerical nature but requires the use of independent judgment.

D. Elements of the Team Concept
What is involved in teamwork? The component parts are:
1. Members
2. A leader
3. Goals
4. Plans
5. Cooperation
6. Spirit

E. Principles of Organization
1. A team member must know what his job is.
2. Be sure that the nature and scope of a job are understood.
3. Authority and responsibility should be carefully spelled out.
4. A supervisor should be permitted to make the maximum number of decisions affecting his employees.
5. Employees should report to only one supervisor.
6. A supervisor should direct only as many employees as he can handle effectively.
7. An organization plan should be flexible.

8. Inspection and performance of work should be separate.
9. Organizational problems should receive immediate attention.
10. Assign work in line with ability and experience.

F. The Four Important Parts of Every Job
1. Inherent in every job is the *accountability* for results.
2. A second set of factors in every job is *responsibilities*.
3. Along with duties and responsibilities one must have the *authority* to act within certain limits without obtaining permission to proceed.
4. No job exists in a vacuum. The supervisor is surrounded by key *relationships*.

G. Principles of Delegation
Where work is delegated for the first time, the supervisor should think in terms of these questions:
1. Who is best qualified to do this?
2. Can an employee improve his abilities by doing this?
3. How long should an employee spend on this?
4. Are there any special problems for which he will need guidance?
5. How broad a delegation can I make?

H. Principles of Effective Communications
1. Determine the media.
2. To whom directed?
3. Identification and source authority.
4. Is communication understood?

I. Principles of Work Improvement
1. Most people usually do only the work which is assigned to them.
2. Workers are likely to fit assigned work into the time available to perform it.
3. A good workload usually stimulates output.
4. People usually do their best work when they know that results will be reviewed or inspected.
5. Employees usually feel that someone else is responsible for conditions of work, workplace layout, job methods, type of tools/equipment, and other such factors.
6. Employees are usually defensive about their job security.
7. Employees have natural resistance to change.
8. Employees can support or destroy a supervisor.
9. A supervisor usually earns the respect of his people through his personal example of diligence and efficiency.

J. Areas of Job Improvement
The areas of job improvement are quite numerous, but the most common ones which a supervisor can identify and utilize are:
1. Departmental layout
2. Flow of work
3. Workplace layout
4. Utilization of manpower
5. Work methods
6. Materials handling

7. Utilization
8. Motion economy

K. Seven Key Points in Making Improvements
1. Select the job to be improved
2. Study how it is being done now
3. Question the present method
4. Determine actions to be taken
5. Chart proposed method
6. Get approval and apply
7. Solicit worker participation

l. Corrective Techniques of Job Improvement
Specific Problems
1. Size of workload
2. Inability to meet schedules
3. Strain and fatigue
4. Improper use of men and skills
5. Waste, poor quality, unsafe conditions
6. Bottleneck conditions that hinder output
7. Poor utilization of equipment and machine
8. Efficiency and productivity of labor

General Improvement
1. Departmental layout
2. Flow of work
3. Work plan layout
4. Utilization of manpower
5. Work methods
6. Materials handling
7. Utilization of equipment
8. Motion economy

Corrective Techniques
1. Study with scale model
2. Flow chart study
3. Motion analysis
4. Comparison of units produced to standard allowance
5. Methods analysis
6. Flow chart and equipment study
7. Down time vs. running time
8. Motion analysis

M. A Planning Checklist
1. Objectives
2. Controls
3. Delegations
4. Communications
5. Resources
6. Manpower

7. Equipment
8. Supplies and materials
9. Utilization of time
10. Safety
11. Money
12. Work
13. Timing of improvements

N. Five Characteristics of Good Directions
In order to get results, directions must be:
1. Possible of accomplishment
2. Agreeable with worker interests
3. Related to mission
4. Planned and complete
5. Unmistakably clear

O. Types of Directions
1. Demands or direct orders
2. Requests
3. Suggestion or implication
4. volunteering

P. Controls
A typical listing of the overall areas in which the supervisor should establish controls might be:
1. Manpower
2. Materials
3. Quality of work
4. Quantity of work
5. Time
6. Space
7. Money
8. Methods

Q. Orienting the New Employee
1. Prepare for him
2. Welcome the new employee
3. Orientation for the job
4. Follow-up

R. Checklist for Orienting New Employees   Yes   No
1. Do you appreciate the feelings of new employees when they first report for work?   ___   ___
2. Are you aware of the fact that the new employee must make a big adjustment to his job?   ___   ___
3. Have you given him good reasons for liking the job and the organization?   ___   ___
4. Have you prepared for his first day on the job?   ___   ___
5. Did you welcome him cordially and make him feel needed?   ___   ___

	Yes	No

6. Did you establish rapport with him so that he feels free to talk and discuss matters with you? ___ ___
7. Did you explain his job to him and his relationship to you? ___ ___
8. Does he know that his work will be evaluated periodically on a basis that is fair and objective? ___ ___
9. Did you introduce him to his fellow workers in such a way that they are likely to accept him? ___ ___
10. Does he know what employee benefits he will receive? ___ ___
11. Does he understand the importance of being on the job and what to do if he must leave his duty station? ___ ___
12. Has he been impressed with the importance of accident prevention and safe practice? ___ ___
13. Does he generally know his way around the department? ___ ___
14. Is he under the guidance of a sponsor who will teach the right way of doing things? ___ ___
15. Do you plan to follow-up so that he will continue to adjust successfully to his job? ___ ___

S. Principles of Learning
  1. Motivation
  2. Demonstration or explanation
  3. Practice

T. Causes of Poor Performance
  1. Improper training for job
  2. Wrong tools
  3. Inadequate directions
  4. Lack of supervisory follow-up
  5. Poor communications
  6. Lack of standards of performance
  7. Wrong work habits
  8. Low morale
  9. Other

U. Four Major Steps in On-The-Job Instruction
  1. Prepare the worker
  2. Present the operation
  3. Tryout performance
  4. Follow-up

V. Employees Want Five Things
  1. Security
  2. Opportunity
  3. Recognition
  4. Inclusion
  5. Expression

W. Some Don'ts in Regard to Praise
1. Don't praise a person for something he hasn't done.
2. Don't praise a person unless you can be sincere.
3. Don't be sparing in praise just because your superior withholds it from you.
4. Don't let too much time elapse between good performance and recognition of it

X. How to Gain Your Workers' Confidence
Methods of developing confidence include such things as:
1. Knowing the interests, habits, hobbies of employees
2. Admitting your own inadequacies
3. Sharing and telling of confidence in others
4. Supporting people when they are in trouble
5. Delegating matters that can be well handled
6. Being frank and straightforward about problems and working conditions
7. Encouraging others to bring their problems to you
8. Taking action on problems which impede worker progress

Y. Sources of Employee Problems
On-the-job causes might be such things as:
1. A feeling that favoritism is exercised in assignments
2. Assignment of overtime
3. An undue amount of supervision
4. Changing methods or systems
5. Stealing of ideas or trade secrets
6. Lack of interest in job
7. Threat of reduction in force
8. Ignorance or lack of communications
9. Poor equipment
10. Lack of knowing how supervisor feels toward employee
11. Shift assignments

Off-the-job problems might have to do with:
1. Health
2. Finances
3. Housing
4. Family

Z. The Supervisor's Key to Discipline
There are several key points about discipline which the supervisor should keep in mind:
1. Job discipline is one of the disciplines of life and is directed by the supervisor.
2. It is more important to correct an employee fault than to fix blame for it.
3. Employee performance is affected by problems both on the job and off.
4. Sudden or abrupt changes in behavior can be indications of important employee problems.
5. Problems should be dealt with as soon as possible after they are identified.
6. The attitude of the supervisor may have more to do with solving problems than the techniques of problem solving.
7. Correction of employee behavior should be resorted to only after the supervisor is sure that training or counseling will not be helpful.

8. Be sure to document your disciplinary actions.
9. Make sure that you are disciplining on the basis of facts rather than personal feelings.
10. Take each disciplinary step in order, being careful not to make snap judgments, or decisions based on impatience.

AA. Five Important Processes of Management
1. Planning
2. Organizing
3. Scheduling
4. Controlling
5. Motivating

BB. When the Supervisor Fails to Plan
1. Supervisor creates impression of not knowing his job
2. May lead to excessive overtime
3. Job runs itself—supervisor lacks control
4. Deadlines and appointments missed
5. Parts of the work go undone
6. Work interrupted by emergencies
7. Sets a bad example
8. Uneven workload creates peaks and valleys
9. Too much time on minor details at expense of more important tasks

CC. Fourteen General Principles of Management
1. Division of work
2. Authority and responsibility
3. Discipline
4. Unity of command
5. Unity of direction
6. Subordination of individual interest to general interest
7. Remuneration of personnel
8. Centralization
9. Scalar chain
10. Order
11. Equity
12. Stability of tenure of personnel
13. Initiative
14. Esprit de corps

DD. Change

Bringing about change is perhaps attempted more often, and yet less well understood, than anything else the supervisor does. How do people generally react to change? (People tend to resist change that is imposed upon them by other individuals or circumstances.

Change is characteristic of every situation. It is a part of every real endeavor where the efforts of people are concerned.

1. Why do people resist change?
   People may resist change because of:
   a. Fear of the unknown
   b. Implied criticism
   c. Unpleasant experiences in the past
   d. Fear of loss of status
   e. Threat to the ego
   f. Fear of loss of economic stability

2. How can we best overcome the resistance to change?
   In initiating change, take these steps:
   a. Get ready to sell
   b. Identify sources of help
   c. Anticipate objections
   d. Sell benefits
   e. Listen in depth
   f. Follow up

II. Brief Topical Summaries

   A. Who/What is the Supervisor?
      1. The supervisor is often called the "highest level employee and the lowest level manager."
      2. A supervisor is a member of both management and the work group. He acts as a bridge between the two.
      3. Most problems in supervision are in the area of human relations, or people problems.
      4. Employees expect: Respect, opportunity to learn and to advance, and a sense of belonging, and so forth.
      5. Supervisors are responsible for directing people and organizing work. Planning is of paramount importance.
      6. A position description is a set of duties and responsibilities inherent to a given position.
      7. It is important to keep the position description up-to-date and to provide each employee with his own copy.

   B. The Sociology of Work
      1. People are alike in many ways; however, each individual is unique.
      2. The supervisor is challenged in getting to know employee differences. Acquiring skills in evaluating individuals is an asset.
      3. Maintaining meaningful working relationships in the organization is of great importance.
      4. The supervisor has an obligation to help individuals to develop to their fullest potential.
      5. Job rotation on a planned basis helps to build versatility and to maintain interest and enthusiasm in work groups.
      6. Cross training (job rotation) provides backup skills.

7. The supervisor can help reduce tension by maintaining a sense of humor, providing guidance to employees, and by making reasonable and timely decisions. Employees respond favorably to working under reasonably predictable circumstances.
8. Change is characteristic of all managerial behavior. The supervisor must adjust to changes in procedures, new methods, technological changes, and to a number of new and sometimes challenging situations.
9. To overcome the natural tendency for people to resist change, the supervisor should become more skillful in initiating change.

C. Principles and Practices of Supervision
1. Employees should be required to answer to only one superior.
2. A supervisor can effectively direct only a limited number of employees, depending upon the complexity, variety, and proximity of the jobs involved.
3. The organizational chart presents the organization in graphic form. It reflects lines of authority and responsibility as well as interrelationships of units within the organization.
4. Distribution of work can be improved through an analysis using the "Work Distribution Chart."
5. The "Work Distribution Chart" reflects the division of work within a unit in understandable form.
6. When related tasks are given to an employee, he has a better chance of increasing his skills through training.
7. The individual who is given the responsibility for tasks must also be given the appropriate authority to insure adequate results.
8. The supervisor should delegate repetitive, routine work. Preparation of recurring reports, maintaining leave and attendance records are some examples.
9. Good discipline is essential to good task performance. Discipline is reflected in the actions of employees on the job in the absence of supervision.
10. Disciplinary action may have to be taken when the positive aspects of discipline have failed. Reprimand, warning, and suspension are examples of disciplinary action.
11. If a situation calls for a reprimand, be sure it is deserved and remember it is to be done in private.

D. Dynamic Leadership
1. A style is a personal method or manner of exerting influence.
2. Authoritarian leaders often see themselves as the source of power and authority.
3. The democratic leader often perceives the group as the source of authority and power.
4. Supervisors tend to do better when using the pattern of leadership that is most natural for them.
5. Social scientists suggest that the effective supervisor use the leadership style that best fits the problem or circumstances involved.
6. All four styles—telling, selling, consulting, joining—have their place. Using one does not preclude using the other at another time.

7. The theory X point of view assumes that the average person dislikes work, will avoid it whenever possible, and must be coerced to achieve organizational objectives.
8. The theory Y point of view assumes that the average person considers work to be a natural as play, and, when the individual is committed, he requires little supervision or direction to accomplish desired objectives.
9. The leader's basic assumptions concerning human behavior and human nature affect his actions, decisions, and other managerial practices.
10. Dissatisfaction among employees is often present, but difficult to isolate. The supervisor should seek to weaken dissatisfaction by keeping promises, being sincere and considerate, keeping employees informed, and so forth.
11. Constructive suggestions should be encouraged during the natural progress of the work.

E. Processes for Solving Problems
1. People find their daily tasks more meaningful and satisfying when they can improve them.
2. The causes of problems, or the key factors, are often hidden in the background. Ability to solve problems often involves the ability to isolate them from their backgrounds. There is some substance to the cliché that some persons "can't see the forest for the trees."
3. New procedures are often developed from old ones. Problems should be broken down into manageable parts. New ideas can be adapted from old one.
4. People think differently in problem-solving situations. Using a logical, patterned approach is often useful. One approach found to be useful includes these steps:
   a. Define the problem
   b. Establish objectives
   c. Get the facts
   d. Weigh and decide
   e. Take action
   f. Evaluate action

F. Training for Results
1. Participants respond best when they feel training is important to them.
2. The supervisor has responsibility for the training and development of those who report to him.
3. When training is delegated to others, great care must be exercised to insure the trainer has knowledge, aptitude, and interest for his work as a trainer.
4. Training (learning) of some type goes on continually. The most successful supervisor makes certain the learning contributes in a productive manner to operational goals.
5. New employees are particularly susceptible to training. Older employees facing new job situations require specific training, as well as having need for development and growth opportunities.
6. Training needs require continuous monitoring.
7. The training officer of an agency is a professional with a responsibility to assist supervisors in solving training problems.

8. Many of the self-development steps important to the supervisor's own growth are equally important to the development of peers and subordinates. Knowledge of these is important when the supervisor consults with others on development and growth opportunities.

G. Health, Safety, and Accident Prevention
1. Management-minded supervisors take appropriate measures to assist employees in maintaining health and in assuring safe practices in the work environment.
2. Effective safety training and practices help to avoid injury and accidents.
3. Safety should be a management goal. All infractions of safety which are observed should be corrected without exception.
4. Employees' safety attitude, training and instruction, provision of safe tools and equipment, supervision, and leadership are considered highly important factors which contribute to safety and which can be influenced directly by supervisors.
5. When accidents do occur, they should be investigated promptly for very important reasons, including the fact that information which is gained can be used to prevent accidents in the future.

H. Equal Employment Opportunity
1. The supervisor should endeavor to treat all employees fairly, without regard to religion, race, sex, or national origin.
2. Groups tend to reflect the attitude of the leader. Prejudice can be detected even in very subtle form. Supervisors must strive to create a feeling of mutual respect and confidence in every employee.
3. Complete utilization of all human resources is a national goal. Equitable consideration should be accorded women in the work force, minority-group members, the physically and mentally handicapped, and the older employee. The important question is: "Who can do the job?"
4. Training opportunities, recognition for performance, overtime assignments, promotional opportunities, and all other personnel actions are to be handled on an equitable basis.

I. Improving Communications
1. Communications is achieving understanding between the sender and the receiver of a message. It also means sharing information—the creation of understanding.
2. Communication is basic to all human activity. Words are means of conveying meanings; however, real meanings are in people.
3. There are very practical differences in the effectiveness of one-way, impersonal, and two-way communications. Words spoken face-to-face are better understood. Telephone conversations are effective, but lack the rapport of person-to-person exchanges. The whole person communicates.
4. Cooperation and communication in an organization go hand in hand. When there is a mutual respect between people, spelling out rules and procedures for communicating is unnecessary.
5. There are several barriers to effective communications. These include failure to listen with respect and understanding, lack of skill in feedback, and misinterpreting the meanings of words used by the speaker. It is also common

practice to listen to what we want to hear, and tune out things we do not want to hear.
6. Communication is management's chief problem. The supervisor should accept the challenge to communicate more effectively and to improve interagency and intra-agency communications.
7. The supervisor may often plan for and conduct meetings. The planning phase is critical and may determine the success or the failure of a meeting.
8. Speaking before groups usually requires extra effort. Stage fright may never disappear completely, but it can be controlled.

J. Self-Development
1. Every employee is responsible for his own self-development.
2. Toastmaster and toastmistress clubs offer opportunities to improve skills in oral communications.
3. Planning for one's own self-development is of vital importance. Supervisors know their own strengths and limitations better than anyone else.
4. Many opportunities are open to aid the supervisor in his developmental efforts, including job assignments; training opportunities, both governmental and non-governmental—to include universities and professional conferences and seminars.
5. Programmed instruction offers a means of studying at one's own rate.
6. Where difficulties may arise from a supervisor's being away from his work for training, he may participate in televised home study or correspondence courses to meet his self-development needs.

K. Teaching and Training
1. The Teaching Process
Teaching is encouraging and guiding the learning activities of students toward established goals. In most cases this process consists of five steps: preparation, presentation, summarization, evaluation, and application.

   a. Preparation
   Preparation is two-fold in nature; that of the supervisor and the employee. Preparation by the supervisor is absolutely essential to success. He must know what, when, where, how, and whom he will teach. Some of the factors that should be considered are:
   1) The objectives
   2) The materials needed
   3) The methods to be used
   4) Employee participation
   5) Employee interest
   6) Training aids
   7) Evaluation
   8) Summarization

   Employee preparation consists in preparing the employee to receive the material. Probably the most important single factor in the preparation of the employee is arousing and maintaining his interest. He must know the objectives of the training, why he is there, how the material can be used, and its importance to him.

b. Presentation
   In presentation, have a carefully designed plan and follow it. The plan should be accurate and complete, yet flexible enough to meet situations as they arise. The method of presentation will be determined by the particular situation and objectives.

c. Summary
   A summary should be made at the end of every training unit and program. In addition, there may be internal summaries depending on the nature of the material being taught. The important thing is that the trainee must always be able to understand how each part of the new material relates to the whole.

d. Application
   The supervisor must arrange work so the employee will be given a chance to apply new knowledge or skills while the material is still clear in his mind and interest is high. The trainee does not really know whether he has learned the material until he has been given a chance to apply it. If the material is not applied, it loses most of its value.

e. Evaluation
   The purpose of all training is to promote learning. To determine whether the training has been a success or failure, the supervisor must evaluate this learning.
   In the broadest sense, evaluation includes all the devices, methods, skills, and techniques used by the supervisor to keep himself and the employees informed as to their progress toward the objectives they are pursuing. The extent to which the employee has mastered the knowledge, skills, and abilities, or changed his attitudes, as determined by the program objectives, is the extent to which instruction has succeeded or failed.
   Evaluation should not be confined to the end of the lesson, day, or program but should be used continuously. We shall note later the way this relates to the rest of the teaching process.

2. Teaching Methods
   A teaching method is a pattern of identifiable student and instructor activity used in presenting training material.
   All supervisors are faced with the problem of deciding which method should be used at a given time.

   a. Lecture
      The lecture is direct oral presentation of material by the supervisor. The present trend is to place less emphasis on the trainer's activity and more on that of the trainee.

   b. Discussion
      Teaching by discussion or conference involves using questions and other techniques to arouse interest and focus attention upon certain areas, and by doing so creating a learning situation. This can be one of the most

valuable methods because it gives the employees an opportunity to express their ideas and pool their knowledge.

c. Demonstration
The demonstration is used to teach how something works or how to do something. It can be used to show a principle or what the results of a series of actions will be. A well-staged demonstration is particularly effective because it shows proper methods of performance in a realistic manner.

d. Performance
Performance is one of the most fundamental of all learning techniques or teaching methods. The trainee may be able to tell how a specific operation should be performed but he cannot be sure he knows how to perform the operation until he has done so.
As with all methods, there are certain advantages and disadvantages to each method.

e. Which Method to Use
Moreover, there are other methods and techniques of teaching. It is difficult to use any method without other methods entering into it. In any learning situation, a combination of methods is usually more effective than any one method alone.

Finally, evaluation must be integrated into the other aspects of the teaching-learning process.

It must be used in the motivation of the trainees; it must be used to assist in developing understanding during the training; and it must be related to employee application of the results of training.

This is distinctly the role of the supervisor.